The Rest of Your Life

Finding relaxation in a non-stop world

Ems Hancock

RIVER
PUBLISHING

River Publishing & Media Ltd
info@river-publishing.co.uk

Scripture quotations are taken from:

ISBN978-1-908393-77-7
Cover design by www.spiffingcovers.com
Printed in the United Kingdom

Contents

Dedication

This book is dedicated to my three nieces:

To dearest Rosie, Indigo and Olivia,
All nieces are brilliant and beautiful
and obviously take after their Aunts.
This book is dedicated to you all,
with the prayer that you will grow up to
know the deep peace of Jesus in your lives.

Love from Auntie Ems x

Acknowledgements

Father God, thank You for helping me tell some of the beautiful story of rest here. I love that You lead me to quiet water and restore my soul.

Thank you again to Tim, my friend and publisher, for your continued belief in me and for your encouragement of my work. The way you run River, centred primarily on revelation and prayer inspires and wows me. I'm honoured to be on your team.

Thank you to my husband, Jon, for standing with me in this crazy season of learning about rest in the wind and the waves. Your ability to sleep through thunder (both metaphorically and literally) awes me. You never sweat the small stuff. You have greater capacity and more peace than any other human I know.

To darling Sam, Ben, Tom and Esther – my four little leaders. Life with you guys is always a fun adventure! You spur me on, teach me, tell me I can achieve anything and give me space to grow and make mistakes as a mummy. I love you!

To our pals, Ian and Jen and Andy and Lucy, thank you all for always knowing what to say, when to say it and when to just bring round a massive meal and a hug the size of Poland. Our joint glorious friendship truly shapes me.

To my siblings without rivalry. Barnes, Dan and Joel. You guys are so awesome. I couldn't be more proud of you. Thank you for always loving your little sis. And thank you for choosing such great wives to be cheerleaders to us all. Thank you Bethie, Sam and Eva for your love and faithfulness to us and especially for your friendship to me.

Thank you to Dad and Stephanie – and Jon's family: Ann, Paul, James and Gran Mae – for the constant bedrock of your love, prayers and support. I am proud to be a Rookwood and a Hancock.

Thank you those who have contributed their wisdom to this book – especially Alice and Paul Belton, Andy Smith, Tina Mann, Emma and Robert Varnam and Lucy Hasler. I am so grateful for your friendship and your insights.

Finally, to everyone at Ivy Church Manchester – especially Anthony and Zoe for creating such a wonderful atmosphere for us all to hear from God and be world-changers. Thank you to all the gang at Ivy Fuse – sneaky shout out to Pete and Lauren! Thank you Ivy Church for filling my heart and my Whatsapp feed; for being both my family and my friends. I love how God has used you all to build me up, champion me and give me so many opportunities to laugh, love and learn over the last 8 years.

Introduction

The still small voice

Hello.

You may be reading this because you can't remember the last time you felt "rested". Perhaps someone has given you this book (or super casually left it on your windscreen), because they are worried about how hard you are working? If so, take the hint my friend. Don't operate any heavy machinery for the next few minutes, assume a seated position, attach slippers and give yourself full permission to relax.

There.

See?

That's better already.

Or, maybe you are concerned about yourself and you're reaching out to this book for a bit of a fresh start? Could it be that you've had that nagging feeling that something is missing from the rhythm and balance of your life and you need to address it? Maybe you've tried Matcha tea, hot yoga, extreme pattern colouring books and mindfulness, but nothing has made you feel less exhausted?

Whatever has brought you here, you are oh-so welcome! Do your best to shut out all the distractions around you. The dishwasher can wait. That email you need to send can be done later. Have I got your full attention? Good.

Soul food

Let me start by asking you something: when was the last time you invested in yourself? (I don't mean when you last got your hair done or took a City and Guilds course in Spot Welding). I mean, when was the last time that you invested in your *soul*?

You might find that a bizarre concept if you are not a person of faith. But the truth is, you do have a soul. The proof of this is at the very point of death. I have seen a number of people after they have passed away. Their body is intact, but their soul has most definitely departed. The unique person they were is no longer there. This is because the soul is eternal. It lives forever. And at the moment of death, it goes to its new home.

There is a great deal to be said for investing in the body. We need to eat the right things, exercise, and drink enough water, but we often neglect the soul – the only part of ourselves that lasts forever. Your soul and mine need feeding. Our souls need nourishment in order to help us function at our best.

This book is a *soul investment*. It is about deep breaths for the very fibre of your being and setting up good patterns to restore the balance of your inner life.

As a Christian, I genuinely find the answers to my questions in the person of Jesus and in God's words as revealed in the Bible. You might think that sounds a bit glib. But it is my experience that both the Old and New Testament are full to the brim of truth, challenge and comfort, that His spirit can help us make sense of, personally. So, if you are tired, stressed and frazzled, the Bible is a great place to look for answers as to why, and suggestions for how God can help you. I hope to prod you in the right direction throughout the following pages.

In Scripture, God reveals Himself in many different ways. One of His most striking of personal encounters ended in a "still, small voice" (see 1 Kings 19:11-14).

If God suddenly decided to speak to you in that way, be honest. Would you hear it? Or would you have life "on too loud" to even notice?

Almost everyone I know is borderline-exhausted. This includes some of my best friends. Severe tiredness and stress have become the norm. Weary parents pad from the school run to work and back again. Exhausted staff set the snooze button and turn up for work just after the meeting has started. There is a lack of play. There are few boundaries where people are truly OFF work, OFF grid or OFF line. And the "crazy" in our worlds is not the good kind.

This is not how we were designed to live!

So, what are we getting wrong? What is missing?

I think rest has become a luxury.

It has grown into something we don't feel we deserve. We feel we can't afford it. No time. No space. No way. That's big.

It's also a lie. Rest is not a luxury. It's not caviar or expensive champagne that we can forgo and simply do without. It's a built-in physical, mental and spiritual requirement. Rest is, and always has been, a necessity that we MUST make space for in our lives. Scary things can happen when we don't rest. I have seen that for myself.

The prince of this world, our enemy, the devil, wars against us resting. Don't get me wrong. He LOVES full-on laziness. That is just evading responsibility and that is the beginning of most of our problems. But he fights against our restfulness. Why? Because he knows how GOOD it is for us. He knows that rest connects us back to God. It reminds us of joy. It helps us be more creative, taps us back into Heaven's perspective and allows us to feel wonderfully free. Of course, he hates it! So, he uses some techniques to keep us in a place of *busy*. He tells us some lies.

Lie number one is based on *deception*. It screams, "I don't need to rest!"

Lie number two is founded on *distraction*. It shouts, "I can't rest until I have done x and y."

Lie number three is centred on *displacement*. It whispers, "I can do this INSTEAD of resting and it will be enough."

I have a problem with all of those statements.

The truth is, I am happier, kinder, more alive and more efficient when I am rested. You are too. But crucially, when I am resting well, I am also more like Jesus.

If you believe that you could embrace more rest in your life and need to know what that could look like for you personally, this book is just for you.

Can I invite you to turn off the noise, shut the screen (unless you are on a Kindle reading this, in which case I let you off and heartily encourage your diligent continuance) and... breathe.

Time to feed that soul of yours.

Chapter 1

Under a Rest

"Almost everything will work again if you unplug it for a few
minutes, including you."
Anne Lamott

Taking rest seriously

One of our friends is a hugely talented TV presenter. My husband
made a show with him a number of years ago and I regularly
went on set to visit both the cast and crew. As the rehearsals
progressed, we noticed our friend doing something I have never
forgotten. During the first couple of days, he brought in a one-
man tent and a sleeping bag. Then, in an unused corner of the
very large studio, away from the sound desk, the cameras and
the noise, he quietly proceeded to pitch his small shelter. During
breaks he would go in, zip it up, and have a restorative little nap!
The art department soon caught wind of what he was doing
and began to build wonderful things around him. It wasn't long
before the tent sported a welcome mat, some bespoke bunting,
toadstools, fairy lights, artificial grass and a whole garden
of flowers and plants! I believe at one time a sizeable garden
gnome may have also appeared.

The creative team made a magical, miniature world for him to escape into each day. He had so much energy and life during the filming and I am convinced that this wonderful little hideaway, where he went to rest every lunch hour, contained part of the reason. He took his rest seriously and therefore so did everyone else on set. In fact, they worked together to playfully and skillfully build the environment for that rest to happen. If visitors came into the studio they were ushered past the tiny garden in hushed and reverent tones.

Our rest is precious. It needs to be taken seriously and built into our days and weeks but, as this story so well illustrates, it should not be without an element of fun and creativity. I am not suggesting you need to rock up at work with a garden gnome and an all-weather sleeping bag in your lunch box... but perhaps there is room for more deliberate, intentional rest in your busy life?

I love the pure and wonderful wisdom of what Philippians 4:12-13 (AMP) says:

"I know how to get along and live humbly [in difficult times], and I also know how to enjoy abundance and live in prosperity. In any and every circumstance I have learned the secret [of facing life], whether well-fed or going hungry, whether having an abundance or being in need. I can do all things [which He has called me to do] through Him who strengthens and empowers me [to fulfill His purpose—I am self-sufficient in Christ's sufficiency; I am ready for anything and equal to anything through Him who infuses me with inner strength and confident peace].

Is there a need for more deliberate calm and quiet contentment in your week? Do you know the secret of facing life in every circumstance, feeling strengthened and empowered with inner strength and confident peace? If I am honest, it is something I can really struggle with.

One of my best friends sent me a text the other day – in response to a rather harassed one from me – that made me laugh. It said, "Sometimes I'm like, 'Where is the cryogenic freeze chamber? I just need a few things to pause for a minute!'"

Ever felt the same?!

Our personal worlds are so fast-paced that we can feel as though we are constantly battling fatigue. Not perhaps from the physical labour that our ancestors dealt with, but from the mental gymnastics we endure to try and stay ahead of the game. Sometimes, without realising it, we are overstimulated by the almost constant noise: social media, TV, advertising, the pressures of work, church and family life. In short, we can find the frenetic pace of our everyday life entirely overwhelming.

I don't know about you, but as a busy mum, even my quiet time (the portion of my early morning when I try and read the Bible and pray) can be far from quiet. In the middle of mine today, my 7-year- old daughter arrived rather breathlessly with what looked like about 30 pairs of clean knickers in a huge pile. She dumped them on my bed and said, "Not one of these fit me Mummy! They are all too tight." DRAMA! Then one of my twins came in and asked me a question about why I *still* (this word was emphasised) hadn't bought him a gum shield for rugby. Suddenly it felt hard to concentrate on the passage in Ezekiel I was trying to study.

Sometimes my body can look still, but my mind is far from it. The inner workings of my brain are pacing and racing as the "to do" list in my consciousness urgently scribbles a few more late entries. I think Rick Warren was spot on when he said, "I could imagine God saying to a lot of us, 'Hey, I'm God, and you're not. You're not the general manager of the universe.'" I know that I need reminding of that! Do you?

Sick and tired

I believe that our society – and even some of our churches – take rest too lightly. We totally underestimate its importance in our lives. Perhaps, at its worst, rest has become seen as something only weak or ill people need and is frowned upon as an expensive indulgence by those who spend each day working and eating "al-desko". A recent online survey, "The Rest Test", carried about by researchers at Durham University, asked more than 18,000 people from 134 countries about their rest patterns and needs. The results showed that 68 percent of people felt that they did not get enough relaxation in their lives. That does not surprise me.

As Alex Soojung-Kim Pang explains in his compelling book *Rest – why you get more done when you work less*, many of us are interested in how to work better, but we don't pay much attention to resting more effectively.

Pang says:

"With a few notable exceptions, today's leaders treat stress and overwork as a badge of honour, brag about how little they sleep and how few vacation days they take, and have their reputations as workaholics carefully tended by publicists and corporate PR firms."

This kind of viewpoint is common in all walks of life. From CEO's to train drivers, pastors to chefs, so many people are rushing around trying to look busy. Busyness says, "Look at me! Notice my worth! I am important! I am needed! I am able! I am competent! I am valuable!"

So, we sit up and take notice. We defer to busy. We become even more busy. We honour busy. We shut out rest. We work longer hours. We sleep less. We drink more coffee, swallow more sleeping pills and then we try to do it all...over... again.

Our society so often defines people by what they do. So, when a person is "doing nothing", they can feel a sense of shame, guilt or inadequacy during those periods. Some of us are terrified of people thinking we are slothful or lazy.

But the truth is, we are just as loved by God when we are resting. We are just as whole, just as precious and just as saved. These feelings of internal poverty are not what our Heavenly Father intended for us as His creation.

The genius of Genesis
Adam's first day on earth was not spent at the office madly printing out spreadsheets or writing projection forecasts. Nor was he busy planting seeds, counting snakes and tending to the animals. He was created, then he and Eve and God all put their feet up! Their first day on was a day off (see Genesis 2:2-3).

What does that tell you?

It tells me that God didn't define Adam by his usefulness. That gives me confidence that God doesn't judge me by my productivity or my CV either. What a relief that is! God doesn't value me or love me because of the fact that I can work. He doesn't think that just because I once had a short-lived role teaching Asian women aerobics or that I recently had a part-time job training telephone engineers to sing in 3-part harmony that I deserve more of His time and attention.

No. He loves me because He made me.

Even my faith is a gift given to me. In truth, nothing about Christianity depends on me, except a willingness to believe that it doesn't depend on me! That makes me smile. (And makes my CV seem a whole lot less vital and my busyness look a lot more... well, pointless).

As we will see later in this book, rest is designed to be so much more than a physical necessity or an inconvenience that stops us being productive workers. It is something that God intended primarily as "GOOD" for me and for you. And because He designed it and it's so beneficial for us, we shouldn't feel guilty when we take time out. More than this, we should relish it, plan it and make time for it.

The rhythm of rest

In a world where we are surrounded by "Get more done!" life hacks, often encouraging weird, borderline-eccentric habits, our need for rest has become less of a focus. One tip I read recently encouraged the use of a timer to break work down into ten minute chunks. Can you imagine trying to produce anything meaningful with an oven timer clicking away on your desk like some nervous, staccato time bomb? I would go into panic mode and make a huge amount of errors! I personally can't think of anything less likely to help me produce creative, meaningful work.

So why is our rest so threatened?

The problem is that many people see rest as simply an absence of work, or as ourselves being "turned off". But this robs rest of its power and strength. Rest is not just a negative vacuum – a way of counting the hours before work starts up again. A person doing this is not resting from work in their mind or body at all.

If we see rest and work as opposites, by very definition they are in opposition to one another. They FIGHT. This is unhelpful. We have to learn to see them as friends that need one another in order to function. We need to realise that we are just as alive when we are resting. The fact is, we need to rest well in order to live well. We also need to rest efficiently to work effectively. It's a circular pattern that requires deliberate and intentional rhythm. As Zimbabwean author, Innocent Mwatsikesimbe says,

"We need work as much as we need rest; the two complement each other, one drawing power and enjoyability from the other. Rest is sweet after work, and work enjoyable after a good rest."

But even from an early age, we push against the wisdom of this. In our house, for example, just the mention of the word "bedtime" can bring on all sorts of creative procrastinations! The phrase, "I just need to..." followed by some plausible excuse for NOT going upstairs, has become one skillfully employed by all four of my kids. They battle with us to stay up longer. Why? Because they see sleep or rest as the enemy of having fun. But rest can be just the opposite. It can be beautiful, wonderful, powerful and (as I have said to my own offspring, more than once), it enables us to have more fun tomorrow. Sleep and rest are restorative and life giving. CS Lewis wrote in one of his letters that he loved the feeling of preparing for sleep. "To curl up warmly in a nice warm bed, in the lovely darkness. That is so restful." I agree. I love my sleep!

Wonderfully, God designed us to need rest and sleep. In fact, this is what He built into us at the very start. Scientists call it the *Circadian rhythm*, but it is basically how God designed the whole universe. Each of us has a 24-hour internal clock breathed into our beings that is running in the background of our brains. It is also known as our sleep/wake cycle. Controlled by part of our *hypothalamus* (a section of our brain) our circadian rhythm works best when we have regular sleep habits, like going to bed at night and waking up in the morning around the same time each day (even including weekends).

God built that requirement into you before you were even thought of. He knew that you would need to rest and to work in a cycle. So, He expertly timed it to coincide harmoniously, both with the days and the seasons. He created periods of darkness to enable you to sleep well and intervals of lighter times to help you to work, rest or play. How wonderful that you and I are built to need and deserve time off!

Are you with me so far?

Now, let's look at some of the reasons we need to relax.

Why should we rest?

1. Rest is biblical. In the book of Exodus God established rest as a command. Up there with "Do not kill", it is built into the order of creation. We know, therefore, that our Father God takes it seriously! Let's read together what He tells us through Moses, in Exodus 20:8-11. In The Message version we see:

> "Observe the Sabbath day, to keep it holy. Work six days and do everything you need to do. But the seventh day is a Sabbath to God, your God. Don't do any work—not you, nor your son, nor your daughter, nor your servant, nor your maid, nor your animals, not even the foreign guest visiting in your town. For in six days God made Heaven, Earth, and sea, and everything in them; he rested on the seventh day. Therefore, God blessed the Sabbath day; he set it apart as a holy day."

God designed us to need rest. He was specific about not working for one day a week and taking it as a holy or "holi"-day. Some of us just blatantly ignore Him. We keep going, doing and being. As a result, we become like several of the seven dwarfs in Snow White: Grumpy, Dopey and Sneezy!

I love what Maya Angelou wrote about taking a day off in *Wouldn't take nothing for my journey now*. She wrote,

"Every person needs to take one day away. A day in which one consciously separates the past from the future. Jobs, family, employers, and friends can exist one day without any one of us, and if our egos permit us to confess, they could exist eternally in our absence. Each person deserves a day away in which no problems are confronted, no solutions searched for. Each of us needs to withdraw from the cares which will not withdraw from us."

God commanded that we rest on the Sabbath. Then He blessed it. This means He gave it credence, imbued it with majesty and made it special. When we avoid having a Sabbath we miss out on that life-giving, healing blessing.

2. Rest is fun. Rest has a reputation of being about "doing nothing". But it is much more exciting and active than that. It isn't just about blobbing in front of the latest box set and downing a beer. It is connected to playful activity that feeds you and your creativity. In John 10:10 (AMP) Jesus told us that He came to offer us that kind of life, the kind that is full and enjoyable. He said,

"I came that they may have and enjoy life, and have it in abundance [to the full, till it overflows]."

Is this the way you would describe your existence? Does your life feel abundant, full and overflowing with joy? Or has the way you live become mundane, humdrum, boring, predictable and soul-less? Perhaps part of the answer may be a lack of play in your everyday world.

It is my experience that God will often give me my best ideas when I am NOT working. He has given me wonderfully creative thoughts when out running, in the bath, on retreat, or on holiday. At various times He has blessed me with dreams at night which help me reimagine some problem I am facing. It is not always at my desk that I think of what to write next!

How many of your best thoughts come at work and how many arrive, unsolicited, in the shower, or on a walk with your dog, or up a mountain? We can get fractious and frustrated when we are not being creative. Perhaps a lack of creativity is a direct result of a lack of time to listen to the whispers of God? Maybe, like me, you can feel out of sync when you aren't living with the rhythm and balance of frequent rest.

3. Rest connects us back to God. It's taken me a while to fully realise this. But it is true to say that rest is found IN Him. As Psalm 62:1-2 (NIV) says:

"Truly my soul finds rest in God; my salvation comes from him. Truly he is my rock and my salvation; he is my fortress, I will never be shaken."

When we rest, we reconnect back to our Father God and this makes us strong and unshakeable. More than this, when we rest we are also mimicking Him – something that the whole of scripture has as its backbone and its goal.

Ephesians 5:1-2 (NET) says:

> "Therefore, be imitators of God as dearly loved children and live in love, just as Christ also loved us and gave himself for us, a sacrificial and fragrant offering to God."

We are made in God's image and our goal is to become more like Him. He rested on the 7th day not because He was tired (we know God does not get physically weary – see Isaiah 40:28), but because He was modelling something for us to copy.

As Leo Baeck writes:

> "The whole love of the 'Law' has been lavished on and has cherished the Sabbath. As the day of rest, it gives life its balance and rhythm; it sustains the week. Rest is something entirely different from a mere recess, from a mere interruption of work, from not working. A recess is something essentially physical, part of the earthly everyday sphere. Rest, on the other hand, is essentially religious, part of the atmosphere of the divine; it leads us to the mystery, to the depth from which all commandments come, too. It is that which re-creates and reconciles, the recreation in which the soul, as it were, creates itself again and catches the breath of life – that in life which is sabbatical."

A decent day of rest recharges you, makes you happy, healthy and helps your spirit function at its best.

True, deep rest brings the resilience, perspective and peace that I think is sorely lacking in our world. And this is found in the person and character of Jesus. Rest isn't just about a day off, but a day plugged in to Jesus Himself. In Matthew 11:28, we read Jesus's words, "Come to me... I will give you rest." In other words, Jesus is saying here, "I am the source of rest. I AM rest. Come to me to get it."

Why is it then that we try to rest without Him? Why is that we don't include Him in our days off? As Pope Jon Paul II said,

"It is Jesus that you seek when you dream of happiness; He is waiting for you when nothing else you find satisfies you; He is the beauty to which you are so attracted; it is He who provoked you with that thirst for fullness that will not let you settle for compromise; it is He who urges you to shed the masks of a false life; it is He who reads in your heart your most genuine choices, the choices that others try to stifle.

It is Jesus who stirs in you the desire to do something great with your lives, the will to follow an ideal, the refusal to allow yourselves to be ground down by mediocrity, the courage to commit yourselves humbly and patiently to improving yourselves and society, making the world more human and more fraternal."

Isn't that so true and so beautiful?

4. Rest connects us to those we love. Rest time is where families are strengthened and friendships are built. True rest is where celebrations are made and laughter and joy are born. I am not saying for a minute that we can't laugh at work. Of course, we can and must. But there is something very precious about memories made during times with family and friends that can last our whole lives.

As I recollect some of the wonderful memories I have of my

own childhood, many of them are centred around the sacrosanct two weeks we had every year on holiday in the Isle of Man. That annual event punctuated and made sense of the rest of our worlds. So much of who I am, the people I grew close to, and the way I understand God is drawn from those 14 days every August at Post St Mary beach mission. Those summers were carefree days of fun, time on the beach, afternoon teas on the prom and silly games around the port. Evening BBQs and picnics near rockpools with the waves lapping nearby were an almost instant cure to just about every stressful thought in my body. Even now, if I feel very mentally stretched or spiritually empty, the sight and sound of the sea can set me right again.

5. Rest is good for the whole of society. I honestly believe that the foundations the Bible gives us on rest and Sabbath are like medicine that we ignore at our peril. Our society has made it more and more difficult for people to have time off and time out. As I have already written, even some of our churches are notoriously bad at allowing people the space to reconnect with relaxation and rest. I think it should be obligatory for church staff to have a paid 24-hour retreat at least every six months. Why? Because the further away we get from the idea of the Sabbath, the more tired people become, the more stressed they feel and the less connected they are with God's laws and principles for themselves and their own reasons to get up in the morning.

As a result of our lack of rest, we seem to be ill, depressed and fearful. We suffer with lower moods and find ourselves needing to self-medicate in order to function. We try to fit our rest into tiny gaps.

As Wendell Berry cleverly observed:

"People are in an emergency to relax. They long for the peace and quiet of the great outdoors. Their eyes are hungry for the scenes of nature. They go very fast in their boats. They stir the river like a spoon in a cup of coffee. They play their radios loud enough to hear above the noise of their motors. They look neither left nor right."

Perhaps you know someone like this? Or maybe you ARE someone like that.

Writer Angela Patmore wrote in *The Spectator* in February 2017, "What has happened to this 'lion-hearted nation', the progeny of those who survived wars and workhouses? The answer, arguably, is that we have been destabilised by drip-fed suggestions that we are psychologically unwell and cannot cope."

In some ways, I agree with her. I have definitely sometimes witnessed a frightening lack of resilience, strength and fight in many of the people I see. And I am pretty sure that this has been modelled to them by the stressed and ill-equipped society we are all part of. Isaiah 30:15 (AMP) contains both a promise and a warning:

"For the Lord God, the Holy One of Israel has said this, 'In returning [to Me] and rest you shall be saved, In quietness and confident trust is your strength.' But you were not willing."

What is God saying to you and are you willing to listen and act on it?

6. Rest restores optimum human functionality. If you deprive any animal of sleep, even for a short period, it will die. There are biological, physiological, psychological, theological and sociological needs for us to rest. In other words, rest is LOGICAL! Scientists used to think that when we slept, the brain shut down. Now we know that when we sleep at night, our resting brains are far from idle. Our sleep cycle looks like this:

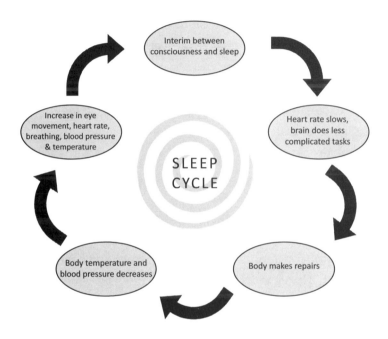

In sleep, our brains go to work consolidating memories, reviewing the events and conversations of the day, and looking for creative solutions to the problems we have faced. As far as you're concerned, you might think you are just "doing nothing", but we now know that sleep improves our physical recovery after exercise. Personal Trainers teach us that muscles are torn in the gym, but rebuilt as we sleep. Did you know that most of your body (not including your bones, teeth or the lenses of your eyes) is replaced every 4 weeks? Especially during rest, your body is constantly renewing itself.

For example, the whole lining of your stomach and gut area is recycled every 1-2 days. And, according to Ana Maria Cuervo of Albert Einstein Medical College, the proteins in your heart are used, repaired, pulped, and recycled every 60-90 minutes. Within every one of your tiny ten trillion cells, there are a staggering billion protein-protein interactions, every single second. You are wonderfully made!

During sleep your brain is being gently and imperceptibly rewired, creating new neural pathways, learning, remembering facts, renewing and remaking your bones and muscle. You are also rapidly growing new skin at a far faster rate than when you're awake.

The truth is that your body is never idle. Every second of your life you are busy producing antibodies, repairing yourself and adapting. Removing rest damages your ability to remember and learn. You also increase your chances of stroke and heart attack, give yourself a higher chance of illness, mess up your skin and even set yourself on a path of weight gain.

People who don't sleep enough appear to produce too much of a hormone known as *ghrelin*. This is associated with feelings of hunger. They also don't produce enough of the hormone *leptin* which tells the body when it is full. Therefore, it is true to say that consistently tired people are at higher risk of obesity.

When we are stressed, we are more likely to eat poorly. Anxiety and fear releases a hormone called *cortisol* that scientists have found to cause cravings, especially for junk foods that are high in fats and sugar. When we are busy, we don't have the time, energy or inclination to eat properly. Perhaps you know this truth for yourself?

Our brains also have great capacity, even when we are not concentrating. Psychologist and memory expert Michael Corballis said in his book *The Wandering Mind – what the brain does when you're not looking*, that, "Mind-wandering is the secret of creativity." Many experiments have been carried out to support this. Even so-called "day dreaming" is not unproductive. It allows us to heighten our imaginations and shift impossibilities to a place of possibility. When we question our routines and imagine change, we restore perspective and open up new ways of thinking.

Studies at Amsterdam University found that people who were given a task to do, and a short puzzle to perform, did better than those who only had one task to concentrate on without the puzzle. Background noise and music has also been proven to stimulate the brain to work more effectively. (Which is why so much work gets done in coffee shops and cafes where the low-level buzz of conversation encourages playful thinking).

So, did you catch that truth? Science shows that we work better when we play during, after and around work.

How incredible is all that?

When I read information like this, I just want to praise God for how wonderfully He has made us! We are intricately built and fabulously designed. But we have a part to play in order to help ourselves function at our best.

The question is this: Is God waiting for you to allow yourself to rest and play more in order to whisper into your conscious or subconscious mind the next dream for your life, your family, your church or your ministry?

Prove it!

Bread needs to be kneaded in order to develop its elasticity. But one of the most important parts of making bread is to rest it. This is process called "proving". The bread is very busy at this stage. It is growing and developing air and space inside itself. It is working on its character and texture. But it has to do this by staying still and, often, by being wrapped up in a warm place. I believe we have lost the art of doing this for ourselves. We rush all over the place getting worked up and tense and then we wonder why we suffer. All we are interested in proving is how hard we work and how late we stay at the office. Perhaps we would be far happier if we had to prove how well we had rested and how much time off we had taken? Wouldn't you love it if your boss handed you a diary and said, "Can you please tell me when you're not going to be here?" That would be something, wouldn't it?! I think Winnie the Pooh was right when he turned to Piglet and said, "Let's start by taking a smallish nap or two."

The priority of rest

I think one of the problems we face is that we wait for the world to grant us the space to rest. And it never comes. Overwhelmed by information (without knowing it), we become saturated in noise, busyness and the clutter of life. How many times do we promise ourselves, "When this busy season is over at work, I will take a day off..."? But that day never comes. The workload stays the same, or in fact, increases. If we do a good job, our bosses load us up with more. They rub their hands and call it "promotion" as a "well done"! But actually, it can feel like more money for less space to be human.

I can promise you something: you are probably not going to magically find a time where your life slows down. Therefore, you need to deliberately practise rest now. It requires discipline and planning. If you want rest, you will have to prioritise it, diary–date-it, and be intentional with it. Rest, like work, is a skill to master not a leftover, bolt-on, optional extra. Like fishing, it requires patience, time, and the ability to catch something that can be pretty slippery.

"The greatest geniuses sometimes accomplish more when they work less." – Leonardo Da Vinci

Rest Reflections:

- Do I recognise my own need for rest?
- Do I prioritise that?
- Am I functioning poorly in any area of my life due to a lack of rest? If so, what could I do differently?
- Do I need God's help to restore some balance in this area of my life?
- Does my work push God and others away from me?
- What will I do as a result of this? What will I pray?

Chapter Two

Who Do You Think You Are?

"The Son of God became a man to enable men to become
sons of God."
CS Lewis, *Mere Christianity*

Killjoy

I am going to be honest with you now. For pretty much the whole
of my adult life I felt guilty when I had time off. More than this,
I also felt rather uncomfortable when other people around me
were having a bit too much fun. I think I had heard one too many
sermons about not letting God find you idle and had somehow
turned that into an idol!

Perhaps, in some ways, my hard work had begun as a lifestyle
choice, but had morphed into an addictive necessity to enable
me to feel worthy of God's attention and love. Deep down I
know I had this mentality. Especially after my Mum died. In the
months following her death I realised all over again that life is
both precious and short. I had a nagging thought in the back of
my mind that I had better not waste any time doing things that
seemed "a bit frivolous". It wasn't that I totally stopped having
any fun (although I almost did), it was the thoughts I had in my

head when I was enjoying myself. At the root of my mind was the ugly sensation of guilt.

But this mindset was challenged early last year when I was listening to a sermon online. The preacher was the American pastor, Joel Osteen. He was talking about how some of us have a "slave mentality". I had heard those kinds of sentiments before, probably many times in church and in various books, but that particular day, I felt God speak to my heart about my own life. I felt Him gently highlighting the way that I felt and the way I was allowing myself to think. It was a bit of a wakeup call. You see, I had been treating myself as though I wasn't really a member of God's *family*, but just part of His *household*. In other words, I had begun to see myself more as a slave than a daughter. I knew I was part of His house, but I thought my place was to simply work hard to please Him. The thought that I *belonged* in His house as someone with ownership, rights and inheritance was one I found uncomfortable and difficult. It was as though grief had masked part of my identity without me even realising it.

Royalty

I remember closing my laptop after hearing this particular talk and just sitting still for a while, trying to process what I was feeling. When we think of ourselves as a slave or servant, we own nothing. We have no privileges. We are, in many ways, "the poor relation", a bit like Fanny Price In Jane Austen's *Mansfield Park*. We do what we are told and keep our heads down.

Imagine for a minute what it's like to live in Buckingham Palace. Apparently, approximately 400 people work there, including servants, chefs, footmen, cleaners, plumbers, gardeners, chauffeurs, electricians, and two people whose sole job it is to look after the rather staggering 300 clocks! Buckingham Palace has a total of 775 rooms, which include 19 state rooms, 52 royal and guest bedrooms, 188 staff bedrooms, 92 offices and a rather implausible 78 bathrooms! I could live there as a servant, but that would be NOTHING like living there as a member of the royal family. As a servant, I would have to be seen and not heard. I would not be able to speak unless spoken to and I would never be allowed to touch a member of royalty. But if I were the daughter of the Queen, my rights would be utterly different. I would be able to go where I liked and do what I liked. Within reason!

Let me explain a bit further. Imagine for a minute that your radiators have failed and you get a plumber in to fix them. You would not expect that guy to let himself in, make his way to your fridge and help himself to a coke. Nor would you be very pleased if he walked into your lounge, kicked off his shoes, sat down on your sofa and popped your TV on. That man is not part of your family. In this instance, he is someone there to do a very specific job for you.

Being a son or daughter is so different. If your child came home and helped themselves to the food and drink in the fridge and turned the TV on, it would be perfectly natural and normal. Your son or daughter has rights and privileges in your home. Why? Because it is THEIR home too. It is where they live and where they belong.

There is something very precious about feeling AT HOME and knowing that we fit into the family. God was showing me through that online talk that I had begun to feel more like a plumber than a princess! I felt I was more involved with fixing leaks and working FOR God, but not doing much WITH Him. Perhaps you know exactly what that feels like?

No longer a slave

The fact is, my identity in Christ is not wrapped up in what I can do for Him. Because I am actually His daughter.

When do we become a son or a daughter? Some might say it is the moment we are born. That very minute you take your first gasp, you have the rights to your father's estate. You own what he owns. Legally. You have done nothing to earn that, except breathe a bit and test out your lungs. You don't have to work to secure that right. It is yours already.

John Wesley, arguably one of the greatest ever preachers, who delivered over 40,000 sermons, put it this way:

"I exchanged the faith of a servant for the faith of a son."

Galatians 4:4-7 (TLB) says,

"But when the right time came, the time God decided on, he sent his Son, born of a woman, born as a Jew, to buy freedom for us who were slaves to the law so that he could adopt us as his very own sons. And because we are his sons, God has sent the Spirit of his Son into our hearts, so now we can rightly speak of God as our dear Father. Now we are no longer slaves but God's own sons. And since we are his sons, everything he has belongs to us, for that is the way God planned."

Isn't that a wonderful truth? Spiritually speaking, I am a "son". Therefore, I have full permission to do all that God's child is permitted to do. I have all His authority, all His power, all His resources and all His wealth at my fingertips. This means I ALSO have His permission to *rest* in total freedom.

I am beginning to learn that living in this kind of freedom doesn't just free me. Conversely, living in emotional bondage won't just tie *me* up in chains; it will also affect the people around me. As Peter Scazzero writes so beautifully and aptly in his blog at *emotionallyhealthy.org*:

> "We free the people we serve. They see a prophetic sign and wonder that we are no longer slaves to work. We are not under powers and principalities of evil (Deuteronomy 5:12-17). Our identity is in God's love and goodness, not what we do.
> ...We communicate, in a different way, that God is on the throne. He is worthy of their trust. During Sabbath rest, God's life also infuses ours in ways that can happen in no other place. After resting, we offer the world something we did not have before. We become a gift."

Wouldn't you like that to happen in your family, your church and your workplace? That you become an emotionally healthy person and a GIFT to others? Shelly Miller wrote in her book, *Rhythms of Rest,*

> "When you abide with God in Sabbath, an unshakable confidence shines from the inside out, enticing others toward the gift of rest as well."

Rest is an open invitation.

Hold your peace

Going back to the Joel Osteen talk I mentioned earlier, God also really spoke to me from the passage he preached from. Do you remember the story in the book of Exodus about Moses asking the leader of Egypt to set the Israelites free? In Exodus 14 we read the account of Pharaoh letting the Israelites go and then changing his mind and chasing after them. When the Hebrews saw the Egyptians giving chase, together with all their chariots and horses, they began to panic (Exodus 14:10). They cried out to the Lord. But Moses told the people:

> "Fear ye not, stand still, and see the salvation of Jehovah, which he will work for you today; for the Egyptians whom ye have seen today, ye shall see them again no more for ever. Jehovah will fight for you, and ye shall hold your peace."
> Exodus 14:13-14 (ASV)

I have deliberately used this older translation of the Bible here because of the language used. Moses told his people not to be afraid, to stand still and watch how God would deliver them. His instruction to them was also to *hold their peace*. Some versions translate that as "be still". But I think being told to "hold your peace" conveys so much more meaning!

We then read the wonderful story of a double deliverance. The people are led through the water and out of slavery for good. Exodus 14:21-22 says:

> "Then Moses stretched out his hand over the sea, and all that night the Lord drove the sea back with a strong east wind and turned it into dry land. The waters were divided, and the Israelites went through the sea on dry ground, with a wall of water on their right and on their left."

Your enemy is dead

This is an amazing rescue! But the rest of the chapter brings EVEN more freedom. It tells the tale of how Pharaoh and his army chased the people into the middle of the sea. God twisted their chariot wheels and threw their forces into total confusion. The Egyptians then wanted to turn back and tried to escape, but before they could, Moses raised his stick again and the waters returned. Not one Egyptian survived.

Can you visualise being there that day to see that truly awful and awesome sight? Can you imagine having to run across the Red Sea with all you possessed, terrified of the raiders behind you? It must have been an utterly terrifying spectacle.

Have you ever thought about why God allowed those Hebrews to see their enemies drown like that?

I think it was to help them to realise that they were truly free. They were not just escaped slaves on the run who could be recaptured and taken back to Egypt at any time. They were *free to be God's people forever* in the land He was taking them to.

In the same way, once we come to know Jesus and receive Him, we are set free from the power of sin and death. We are no longer slaves to fear, or anything else for that matter. In a very real sense we are not simply hired by Him, but we *belong* to Him (see Romans 8:9 and 1 Corinthians 7:4). We are given full rights as children of God and inheritors of the Kingdom.

Free people have privileges, goals, inheritance and dreams. They also have permission to "hold their peace" – as that more ancient version of the Bible declared – and enter into God's rest.

Luke 15 tells us the wonderful story of the Prodigal Son, (something that I dramatise in my book *In Security – living a confident life*). In verses 21-24 we read:

"The son said to him, 'Father, I have sinned against heaven and against you. I am no longer worthy to be called your son.' But the father said to his servants, 'Quick! Bring the best robe and put it on him. Put a ring on his finger and sandals on his feet. Bring the fattened calf and kill it. Let's have a feast and celebrate. For this son of mine was dead and is alive again; he was lost and is found.' So, they began to celebrate."

There is nothing as palpably beautiful as coming home like this. When we come to know Jesus, God restores us from a place of unworthiness to a role of eternal sonship.

One of the most wonderful truths in the whole of the Bible must be this precious verse from Galatians 5:1 which declares the promise that,

> "It is for freedom that Christ has set us free. Stand firm, then, and do not let yourselves be burdened again by a yoke of slavery."

One of the songs I have really loved in this season is *No Longer Slaves* from Bethel Music. The words are beautiful and contain much of the story we've just looked at. If you don't know it, let me encourage you to spend some time looking it up and listening to it. It contains such a powerful set of truths.

Your enemy's power is defeated

There were two girls in my school whose parents were part of the Italian mafia in Liverpool. They hung around with a very cool girl called Ayesha. No one messed with these girls. They were people I tried to avoid. One night I was out in town and they were in the same club. I think I nervously made a joke to one of them. She didn't find it funny. At all. In fact, she took offence. She broke a bottle on the table and came towards me with it. I ran from the club and even left my high-heeled shoes behind. Then I heard her friend was also after me. I heard she was going to "batter me on the bus" on the way home from school. I was very scared. But then, for some reason, Ayesha took my side. Ayesha was a unit. No one crossed her. She told those two other girls not to hurt me. I came under her protection. Nothing ever happened to me.

It is great news to remember the power of the cross and what it achieved for us. Good Friday is good because Jesus died on those planks of wood for our permanent protection. Good Friday is also good because it dealt with our debt. It allowed us the chance to be forgiven and set free. Instead of having to spend life feeling rubbish, guilty and condemned, we get to walk tall, released into a new relationship with God. That first Good Friday at around 3pm, our enemy was defeated! He lost the battle for our lives and he also lost the battle over death and sin. Because of the cross my sin is dealt with, my future is secured, my worst problems are already solved!

Hebrews 10:19-23 (NIV) reminds us,

"Therefore, brothers and sisters, since we have confidence to enter the Most Holy Place by the blood of Jesus, by a new and living way opened for us through the curtain, that is, his body, and since we have a great priest over the house of God, let us draw near to God with a sincere heart and with the full assurance that faith brings, having our hearts sprinkled to cleanse us from a guilty conscience and having our bodies washed with pure water. Let us hold unswervingly to the hope we profess, for he who promised is faithful."

As this passage says, our job now is to draw near to God with a sincere heart and with the full confidence of faith.

What is Sabbath?

The existence of the Sabbath reminds us of freedom, choice, liberty and the wonderful relationship we talked about earlier. But what does Sabbath actually mean and what could it look like today?

The word "Sabbath" translates from the Hebrew noun *shabbat* (שבת). It comes from the verb *shavat* which means "to cease", "to stop working" or "to rest". Sabbath in the Bible specifically refers to doing nothing related to work for 24 hours each week. There are two very extreme ways to approach Shabbat. One is to be incredibly legalistic and be bound by all kinds of rules and laws associated with it. But we need to remember that we are not saved by keeping the Sabbath, but saved by Jesus. Jesus taught us that the Sabbath was made for people, not the other way around (see Mark 2:27). The other extreme is to ignore Shabbat completely as an outdated command.

But there is a more balanced biblical position to hold. Sabbath is a rest discipline that I believe is essential for our spiritual maturity and growth. God doesn't love us more if we do certain things. But not keeping a day of rest is an indicator that we are too busy and taking on too much.

For us in this day and age, taking a Sabbath is about selecting a time period and protecting it. Remember, people who choose to work 7 days a week are essentially still acting like slaves! We need to remember who we are. Some people choose to rest on a Saturday, a Thursday or a Sunday. I don't think it matters which day we choose, but I think it really does matters that we switch off for one whole day a week.

The acceleration of rest

In our church we have a "word of the year", which is something our Pastor waits on God for and will announce in early January. The word will frame the time period, describe something that God will do and sets us up to be expectant for growth and a move of Heaven in that area. In 2017 we found ourselves in the "Year of acceleration". Large numbers of people across our church in Manchester experienced a year where God did new things, faster for them than ever before. Jon, myself and many others, saw new doors of opportunity open, fresh challenges overcome and different ways of working become normal.

Our dear friend Alice spent most of last year discovering this acceleration for herself, but in an unexpected way. When the title of the year was announced, like us, she felt really excited, imagining that her and her husband's business might reach new heights, or that other successes might occur.

But very soon into the year God asked her to stop and slow down. He began to reveal to Alice that she needed to be light in order to accelerate well. A bit like a racing car is built from lightweight but streamlined material, Alice kept sensing God talking to her about shedding different parts of herself which would then allow her to go at His speed. She realised that she had tried to accelerate in her own strength all her life. In prayer, she discovered the truth that she was too busy and that her busyness was causing her to lose her peace. She said,

"For me to really accelerate in my life I had to learn how to shed the weights that I thought made me strong – the weight of doing things in my own power; of proving that I was worth it. I had to stop striving to validate myself in subtle ways; by people-pleasing or comparing and desiring to be 'as good as' or in some cases 'better than' others.

It started by my fasting from social media for the month of

January. And continued with me considering the motivations for my actions. I began saying 'no' to certain things if I felt I was doing them from a place of obligation, or because I wanted people to like me.

I literally had to stop. All I did was cook, look after my family and see friends if they wanted to, but that was IT. I worked hard in my garden, growing wonderful produce, spent time with my family and hours just loving Jesus.

I learnt that not only was this enough for me, it was simply wonderful! By shedding my busyness (which was a painful and challenging process) I became more peaceful. By diving into the peace and tranquillity of God and resting long enough to enjoy it, I experienced my Jesus in deeper and more beautiful depths. He became my true accelerator, not me. For Him to be this I needed to accept my weaknesses and limitations. I had to submit to His power, authority and direction in my life. It was in this process that I became light and fulfilled."

I asked Alice what impact this had on her now. She said,

"I am by no means finished, but I am certainly much lighter. I like myself. I love others more and I have learned how to keep my peace. Also, I would definitely say I experience greater power because, now, I know it's nothing to do with me. It's not mine. Its God's.

This is genuinely the first time in my life I am doing what I feel 'called' to do. I am finally living a life that I love. I'm doing what I have dreamed of for 15 years .... I have accelerated more than I could imagine! By stopping, I started to go faster."

I love this story so much and what it means for our lovely Alice. It reminds me of the wonderful truth found in John 8:36 (NIV):

"So, if the Son sets you free, you will be free indeed."

It is so wonderful to see Alice thriving and growing. Her wisdom has soared in this last year and she has become a person of greater depth and serenity.

In many ways, as we will see in the remainder of the book, rather than holding us back, rest gives us the stability, freedom and energy for what God is calling us towards.

Rest Reflections:

- If someone observed my everyday life, would they see a stressed and fearful slave at work, or a confident child at play?
- Am I treating myself as a slave, even though God says I am His child?
- In what areas of my life am I not truly free? What can I do to address that?
- What rights does a child of God have that I need to pursue more fully?
- How does the knowledge of my inheritance in Christ comfort and bless me? How does it challenge me today?
- What practical things can I stop/start to strengthen my personal awareness and identity of myself as a child of God?
- Which part of Alice's story impacted me the most? What could I do about that? What do I need to pray?

Chapter Three

The Glorification of Busy

"Go to sleep in peace. God is awake."
– Victor Hugo

In the Old Testament we read that there were many articles of furniture in the Tabernacle and that each served a different purpose (see Exodus 25-31). But did you ever notice that there was not a single chair in the whole place? Why? Perhaps it was because the priests never had time to sit down! (Maybe you know how they felt?!) They were so busy, rushing around making sacrifices for the many sins of the people.

However, when Jesus died and went to heaven what do you think the very first thing He did was? You guessed it – it was to sit down (see Mark 16:19, Hebrews 1:3 and 10:12). He knew that His work on earth was complete; that He had paid the price for each of us and that He could relax and enjoy the presence of God, for eternity.

The throne of race
Our schedules are so toxic that we have forgotten what it feels like not to RUSH everywhere. Busyness is not listed in the Bible

as a spiritual gift (!), yet we celebrate it as if it is. We ask how someone is, and when we get a list of the 10 things they have just done, we can feel awed, impressed and even unworthy. But should we?

I bet you have some dreams and goals that you want to achieve. Maybe your list contains things like:

• Learn Spanish
• Visit Thailand
• Lose a stone
• Run 10k

But I wonder if REST MORE would ever make your list? I know that for many of us, it wouldn't even come last! We all have lists of things we would like to do in the next year, in the next week, even in the next day – and that's all well and good. But for so many of us, busyness takes over even our best-laid plans. Our goals can lie unachieved for years because we haven't had the time to even think about them. We are too busy just trying to keep going, spinning all the normal plates of our existence.

Theologian Tryon Edwards said, "Have a time and place for everything, and do everything in its time and place ... you'll not only accomplish more, but have far more leisure than those who are always hurrying."

How does that sit with you? Do you feel as though life passes you by in a whirlwind of activity and busyness, without much to show for it? Are you known as a "hurrier" or a "worrier"? Do your children or your friends feel you are a person who is "at peace"? Or are you constantly tired, chasing your tail, complaining and exhausted?

C.S. Lewis wrote,

"The moment you wake up each morning, all your wishes and hopes for the day rush at you like wild animals. And the first job each morning consists of shoving it all back, in listening to that other voice, taking that other point of view, letting that other, larger, stronger, quieter life come flowing in."

I know that feeling well. If I am honest, there are many times in my own life where the demands on my time seem to reach some kind of epic seismic counter. I buy into the lie that I somehow have to achieve 41 things *before breakfast*. The jobs in my brain crowd out my time with God and squeeze the joy out of my day. As Pastor Shaun Smith said, "It is a temptation to approach God from the throne of race, rather than meeting Him at the throne of grace."

Did you know that the average person lives 77 years, 28,000 days, or 670,000 hours? Yet the average Christian spends less than 10 minutes a day purposefully seeking God? That's equates to less than 6 hours a month, 3 days a year, or less than 7 months in a whole lifetime.

I'm not writing that to guilt you, just to show you how unconnected we all are to the source of our joy, peace and strength. It certainly doesn't seem like a ratio to be proud of, does it?

I love what Paul Maxwell wrote in the *Desiring God* blog:

"Our rest is not measured in minutes or hours, but in proximity. Sabbath is a day, but it is also a place with God – a place He makes, where He pursues us...

Sabbath is not just an interruption of your to-do list – the bullet points that dominate our day. Sabbath is an encounter. And Jesus – the God who separated dry land from the waters

– will mix them together again to create a Sabbath morning and evening in us – with the mud, with our mess – by his initiative."

I speak to people who seem to feel as though the world is resting squarely on their shoulders. Their stress levels are palpably high. The atmosphere around them is tense, pulsing, fraught and a lack of peace reigns. The words that come out of their mouths are clipped, anxious and uptight. This is even the case for those of us who are meant to have "peace that passes understanding" within us. Perhaps, as Dr Lewis Sperry Chafer once said, "Much of our spiritual activity is little more than a cheap anaesthetic to deaden the pain of an empty life."

So, what are the signs of being spiritually undernourished and just plain old "too busy"? The following pages are some of the symptoms we might spot in ourselves or others. And again, I am not writing these to load you up with a sense of shame or self-reproach, but to give you some permission to recognise that perhaps you need to be take stock and be kinder to yourself.

1. Lack of intimacy with God

I recently heard a Bill Johnson sermon online in which he said, "Busyness always wars against our awareness of God." This is so true. Our frantic hurry squashes out time with the creator of our peace. It stands to reason: if peace is found in Him, but we are not, we will not be people of peace, will we? Charles R. Swindoll agreed when he wrote, "God never asked us to meet life's pressures and demands on our own terms or by relying upon our own strength. Nor did He demand that we win His favour by assembling an impressive portfolio of good deeds. Instead, He invites us to enter His rest."

I so need that! I need that rest every single day. I can find myself swamped by the expectations and the cares of life, just like you. I have to choose to surround myself with God's presence and His promises.

James 4:7-8a (NLT) says, "So, humble yourselves before God. Resist the devil, and he will flee from you. Come close to God, and God will come close to you."

Other versions render this truth, "Draw near to God and he will draw near to you."

When was the last time you truly drew near to your Father?

2. Lack of reflection

I know many people who never seem to be happy with their achievements, but the Bible tells us that,

"A desire accomplished is sweet to the soul." (Proverbs 13:19 NKJV)

Perhaps you are someone who doesn't take the time to reflect on what has been done before you rush on to your next obligation? The danger of that is that we can miss the joy of savouring a job completed and well done. Remember that when God created the world, He took time out to label His work GOOD and stood back to admire it for a while (Genesis 1:4). When was the last time you allowed yourself the luxury of basking in a finished piece of work before embarking on the next? I think it is very helpful to have such celebrations and markers in life.

I will offer you a small example. Every time I finish writing a book I buy myself a special cookbook, often by my favourite cook, Mary Berry. I write a note to myself on the flyleaf, marking the occasion. It is my way of being grateful for hard work accomplished and completed. It is a small but personally significant way of signposting the moment. We all need ways to do this for ourselves.

A few years ago, I treated myself to a Bible with a very wide margin. It is now my journalling Bible and means I can draw, write or jot my thoughts down alongside the text. Reading that Bible is now a much richer experience for me. I can see my answered prayers and thoughts, together with the original text.

Having a "margin" or space in life is so key, because it enables reflection, inspires gratefulness and brings hope.

Psalm 1:1-3 (NIV) talks more about what happens when we meditate and medicate our lives with God's words. It says,

"Blessed is the one
who does not walk in step with the wicked
or stand in the way that sinners take
or sit in the company of mockers,
but whose delight is in the law of the Lord,
and who meditates on his law, day and night.
That person is like a tree planted by streams of water,
which yields its fruit in season
and whose leaf does not wither—
whatever they do prospers."

I know many people who feel as though their physical or spiritual "leaves" are withered and whatever they do lacks energy. This set of verses shows us how to be the opposite. Allowing ourselves the time to reflect on and delight in the beauty of God's Word, brings life, prosperity of soul and vitality to our bodies and minds. Are your leaves withering? Perhaps you need to check whether or not you are planted by a stream.

3. Lack of sleep
I am sure we all know the horrible feeling of tossing and turning

in bed and getting up the following day feeling sleep-deprived and grouchy. Our tiredness affects everyone around us as we pass on and perfect that "just got out of bed the wrong side" tone of voice! Our health, our productivity and our grace levels take a nose dive as we feel exhausted. We ALL know it when our children, our partners or our bosses haven't had their full quota of rest.

Writer Roger Zelazny wrote,

"Of all the things a man may do, sleep probably contributes most to keeping him sane. It puts brackets around each day. If you do something foolish or painful today, you get irritated if somebody mentions it, today. If it happened yesterday, though, you can nod or chuckle, as the case may be."

The understanding that sleep puts "brackets around each day" is such a helpful one to consider. Rest does this for us. It gives us the much-needed punctuation, pause and stillness each of us need. If we lie awake, hour after hour, fretting over our problems, our woes won't get any better. In fact, as Diane Setterfield wrote:

"An unrested mind is prone to wander into unfruitful avenues; (but) it is nothing that a good night's sleep cannot cure." It is true that a decent rest can feel like the medicine for many ills. John Steinbeck said, "It is a common experience that a problem difficult at night is resolved in the morning, after the committee of sleep has worked on it."

In Jeremiah 31:25 (ESV) God says to us, "For I will satisfy the weary soul, and every languishing soul I will replenish."

What a wonderful promise that is!

Jesus showed us what it meant to have the perfect balance between rest and activity. He modelled calm trust in the provision and protection of God. Like Jesus, we don't need to lose our own peace or sleep because of fear, anxiety or stress. In sleep, God goes to work on our behalf, fighting our battles and bringing us His life and salvation. Whatever storms we face in life, it is possible to hold on to the truth that God is with us through them.

Psalm 91:4-6 (NKJV) contains these words of comfort and protection:

"He shall cover you with His feathers,
And under His wings you shall take refuge;
His truth shall be your shield and buckler. You shall not be afraid of the terror by night,
Nor of the arrow that flies by day, nor of the pestilence that walks in darkness,
Nor of the destruction that lays waste at noonday."

4. Lack of direction

I know that for much of my life I have been a bit directionless. If someone asked me to do something, and it even vaguely felt like a good idea, or I thought it would bless them, I would do it. The result of this was that I spread myself quite thin. Because I can turn my hand to a number of things (to a certain degree), I found myself leading worship, running kid's church, visiting the elderly, going to missionary prayer meetings, writing songs (for other people's albums), teaching youth group and cooking for church dinners I never got to eat. And some of that was on my days off! I was tempted to follow other people's dreams and passions and even copy their vision, because I wasn't hugely sure of my own calling. Perhaps you know what that feels like?

But a number of years ago, following on from a conference

at church, I realised that I needed to say "no" to certain things in order to be more effective at keeping to the revelation God had given me about my own life. I think I had been wandering around, going from one random thing to another, keeping manically busy, but not feeling centred or purposeful. To be honest, it felt like a minor miracle if I managed to avoid clashing all the crazy activities of each day! I just don't think I had ever been taught that this was far from an ideal way to run my world.

I find it freeing to remember now that *I am not meant to support every charity or help to run every event I hear about*. I am not meant to be at every church activity or give my time and energy to every person who asks me for help. I would never get anything done that God HAS asked me to do if I did this. I have to be prayerful and discerning. If I spend all my energy on things that aren't my anointed gifting, I will stop others from stepping into *their* God-given roles. I will also neglect the tasks God has assigned for me.

A few days ago, a lovely friend of mine asked me to get involved in a new work she was starting. It sounded great. But when I checked it against my own life goals and the things God has been kind enough to reveal to me as my "inheritance words", they simply didn't match up. It was a total disconnect. It was very freeing to be able to explain that whilst I supported her wholeheartedly, I couldn't participate in this particular project.

Another of my wise, close friends explained to me a few weeks ago that there is a real difference between telling someone you are FOR them, but not feel you have to journey WITH them. In other words, you can be *behind* someone spiritually, without being *beside* them physically. How great and helpful is that revelation?

A word of caution on this though: I don't want to be someone selfishly unaware of people's needs and saying "no" to everyone who asks me something. That is not being like Jesus at all. But, neither do I want to be at everyone's beck and call so that I neglect my family, my job, or the work God has prepared for me to do. Ephesians 2:10 (NIV) helps us here. It says, "For we are God's handiwork, created in Christ Jesus to do good works, which God prepared in advance for us to do."

In other words, we are created uniquely by Jesus to do certain things which He has already set out for us. If we are not careful, we could miss that calling, trying to do everyone else's work for them! It can be just as ungodly to say "yes" too much, as it can be to say "no" too frequently. The secret is to get on board with what God is building in your life.

Shauna Niequist puts this so eloquently:

"If you're not careful with your yeses, you start to say no to some very important things without even realising it. In my rampant yes-yes-yes-ing, I said no, without intending to, to rest, to peace, to groundedness, to listening, to deep and slow connection."

Psalm 127:1-2 (NLT) explains this further:

"Unless the LORD builds a house, the work of the builders is wasted. Unless the LORD protects a city, guarding it with sentries will do no good. It is useless for you to work so hard from early morning until late at night, anxiously working for food to eat; for God gives rest to his loved ones."

God needs to be in charge of our calling and our direction. Not people. And the beautiful promise He gives us when we do this, is true REST for us, His loved ones.

5. Lack of boundary

A keynote speaker from Billy Graham ministries was once speaking at a pastor's conference in the US. He caused a stir in the audience when he said, "A busy Christian is not a spiritual Christian." There was a slight buzz around the room as people reacted to his statement. I am sure some of those pastors bristled. Others may have felt a sense of relief. Others may have thought they had heard him wrong.

So much of being in God's presence is about rest and stopping. But many people I know are breathlessly living in a world of last-minute decisions. Heavily relying on their own resources to get them through things that are half-prepared or poorly-conceived, they feel like they are on a runaway train.

When we allow work to bleed into every other area of life it will disrupt the balance and rhythm we are meant to have. All we do for work, both in terms of paid or unpaid activity, needs to have boundary lines. The good news is that the Bible tells us in Psalm 16:5-8 (NIV) that our lives can have helpful, clear and even pleasant borders:

"Lord, you alone are my portion and my cup;
you make my lot secure.
The boundary lines have fallen for me in pleasant places;
surely I have a delightful inheritance.
I will praise the Lord, who counsels me;
even at night my heart instructs me.
I keep my eyes always on the Lord.
With him at my right hand, I will not be shaken."

I think this is really key. When we know what we *don't have to do*, it frees us to do the things we *are meant to do*.

You may want to read that again!

Operating from this place allows us to work better and to rest more effectively.

Psalm 144:14 (CSB) says, "Our cattle will be well fed. There will be no breach in the walls, no going into captivity, and no cry of lament in our public squares."

In a world of terrorism, turmoil and tempestuous politics, this is an amazing prayer and promise! The truth is, when our boundaries are in the wrong place, this brings bondage. We all know people who are working too hard, carrying fear, living with anxiety and wading through stress. They are enslaved, but they can't see it. We read of nation squaring up against nation, leaders unwisely venting their vitriol on Twitter; others sending out test missiles to show their strength. It can feel like a dangerous world to inhabit. Later in Psalm 147:14 we read the truth, "He grants peace to your borders and satisfies you with the finest of wheat."

It is wonderful in all this to remember that God's eyes never shut. He is constantly working on our behalf, even when we are fast asleep (Psalm 121).

6. Lack of exercise

I'm afraid to say that I used to view exercise as a bit of a waste of time, or even as a slight vanity project. But I have learnt, slowly and surely that our bodies are a gift from God that we need to take care of, to the best of our ability. Rick Warren, pastor of Saddleback Church, had an epiphany one day while he was baptising 858 people (that's a long service!) After dipping the 500th body into the water, his arms began to ache. It led him to think he was out of shape. He decided to write a book called *The Daniel Plan* alongside health experts to address the problem. On this plan, he lost over 30 pounds. He said,

"You may have had so many failures at changing the way you eat or exercise or think or act, that the possibility of lasting change feels like an unreachable goal. Well, to be honest with you, it probably will be – unless you plug into God's power. What is impossible from a human standpoint is easy to God. With God, today's impossibility is tomorrow's miracle."

What Rick realised so clearly for himself was that we are stewards of our own bodies. We need to make sure that we look after ourselves well, that we give ourselves good food, exercise, and the chance to develop, grow and honour what God has given us. By being healthy and fit, we are also more able to care for others and carry out our God-given vocations. Proverbs 31:17 (NIV) tells us, "She sets about her work vigorously; her arms are strong for her tasks."

I don't know about you, but I need to be physically strong to carry my load. Like you, I need to lift heavy shopping, move furniture, lug the hoover up and down the stairs and to hug people hard! (People often say I am good hugger, but I train for it!). In my office, I have two sets of weights. Namby pamby ones for days when I feel a bit gentle and achy, and slightly heavier ones for days when I feel like Bear Grylls. Every now and again during the day I will stand up, stretch, and lift a few weights. It does me no end of good!

In Proverbs 24:5 (ESV) we read, "A wise man is full of strength, and a man of knowledge enhances his might."

I have learnt that it is important for me and my family to move often and purposefully. I have the kind of body that likes to be still, but regrets it afterwards. If I sit for too long I get creaky and squeaky! I am learning to be more active in my day-to-day life. Because of my fitness, I have found that everyday chores have become easier and quicker for me to complete. I also find that I am not as tired all the time. Exercise gives me energy to have more capacity. More than this, exercise feeds my creativity.

Exercising regularly can increase our brain capacity, boost our stamina and resilience, and relieve many sources of stress and tension. A German study in 2015 also found that exercise "induces profound structural brain plasticity". In other words, keeping fit makes us more teachable and blesses our brains with the ability to make better connections.

Reggie Love, who served in the Obama administration as the President's special assistant and personal aide, said that Barack Obama's personal physical fitness routines were one of the keys to his success. When on Robben Island, Nelson Mandela used exercise to break up the monotony of his day. Even when he was released from prison he continued with his morning fitness regime.

The satirical comic strip writer, Scott Adams, famed in the USA for his very funny comic character, Dilbert, talks about his need for exercise. After a few hours at his desk, Scott goes to the gym, knowing that, at that point, his brain is only suited for, as he humorously says, "lifting heavy objects and putting them right back where I found them." He also said, "Creativity is not something you can summon on command. The best you can do is set an attractive trap and wait."

I totally subscribe to this idea. For me, there is an undeniably clear link between my exercise and robust thought. Many times, when I have been on a run (or sitting on one of those annoyingly uncomfortable bike things at the gym) I have suddenly come up with a really good idea. I am certain God plants creative thinking in me when I am Lycra clad.

7. Lack of self-care routines

In my work as a school listener I sometimes see young people who I just want to take home. A deep motherly desire rises within me and I have to harness the overwhelming feelings in my heart of wanting to feed them, clothe them and sometimes even to teach them the social values of washing.

Not eating well or practising healthy self-care routines makes us feel low, lacking in energy, and can sometimes even be off-putting for others. You may know someone whose appearance changed after a life event. Perhaps you have a friend who stopped washing their hair as often after their divorce? Or maybe you know someone who "let themselves go" physically after a grief or loss of some kind? Or maybe you know another person who became obsessed with their appearance after some kind of trauma? Our self-care routines are always a clue to how we are feeling about ourselves.

When we are busy, it can be hard to do the very things that help us stay on top. We can find that, all too soon, it's over a month since we went for a run, or its two weeks since we last ate a decent meal. It is easy to get into poor habits. Maybe you have stopped meeting up with the people you pray with because life has got too crazy? Maybe you don't go to church any more? Perhaps you have ceased to give yourself those days out that you need to keep you focused and happy?

The great news is that Jesus gets it!

He cares very much if we are tired. He knows how we are at every moment of our lives. Jesus said,

"Are you tired? Worn out? Burned out on religion? Come to me. Get away with me and you'll recover your life. I'll show you how to take a real rest. Walk with me and work with me

– watch how I do it. Learn the unforced rhythms of grace. I won't lay anything heavy or ill-fitting on you. Keep company with me and you'll learn to live freely and lightly." (Matthew 11:26-30 MSG)

It is likely that I don't know you, but I believe that these words can be a tool that God can use to reach into your heart right now. Maybe you are struggling with anxiety or depression and you can't seem to break free of it? He knows. He cares. He loves you. He is near you.

Last year, I led a family service at our church about Elijah. It was a passage from 1 Kings 19 that, to be honest, I wasn't that familiar with. As I started to prepare my very simple talk, I realised how relevant the passage was for all the people I knew who were struggling with low mood, fatigue, stress, anxiety, fear, depression, panic attacks and exhaustion. Read on to see what I mean:

"When Elijah saw how things were, he ran for dear life to Beersheba, far in the south of Judah. He left his young servant there and then went on into the desert another day's journey. He came to a lone broom bush and collapsed in its shade, wanting in the worst way to be done with it all – to just die: 'Enough of this, GOD! Take my life – I'm ready to join my ancestors in the grave!' Exhausted, he fell asleep under the lone broom bush.

Suddenly an angel shook him awake and said, 'Get up and eat!'

He looked around and, to his surprise, right by his head were a loaf of bread baked on some coals and a jug of water. He ate the meal and went back to sleep.

The angel of GOD came back, shook him awake again, and said, 'Get up and eat some more – you've got a long journey ahead of you.'

He got up, ate and drank his fill, and set out. Nourished by that meal, he walked forty days and nights, all the way to the mountain of God, to Horeb. When he got there, he crawled into a cave and went to sleep." (1 Kings 19: 3-9 MSG)

Did you see anything in those verses that connects with your own experience? If so, know again that God understands your needs today. He knows if you are disappointed, or low. He knows if you cried hard last night. He knows if you feel overwrought, in pain or crushingly lonely.

Perhaps it is time to take more ownership of your life, beginning with some simple self-care? Perhaps you need better food, or more sleep or more time out? Maybe you need to tell Him and others how you are feeling? I explain more what this could look like for you later in the book.

7. Lack of personal discipline

If I'm not careful, I can vascillate between being crazily disciplined and super laid back about everything. I have to try to be balanced in this area. As a writer, I HAVE to discipline myself to sit in a room on my own for hours at a time. I also have to choose to do THIS, rather than the many other things that clamour for my energy and attention. Right now, for example, I am ignoring a great many things on my "To-don't list" in order to devote my thinking towards this paragraph and this page! Why do I do this? Because I know that the discipline of just sitting and writing often yields far greater results for me than waiting for a lightning bolt of creativity to strike. Far from being an enemy of inspiration, routine can fuel inventiveness for me. Writer Anthony Trollope paid a servant an extra £5 a year to wake him at 5am with a coffee. He later said, "I owe more to him than to anyone else for the success I had."

Pablo Picasso is said to have rather brilliantly quipped, "Inspiration exists, but it has to find you working."

I have occasionally been asked how I can write books alongside all the other things in my world. My answer is that God has grown my capacity for the things that are important to Him. But I still have to work at being disciplined. It doesn't come naturally to wake up in the morning and magically arrive at my desk, raring to go.

2 Timothy 1:7 declares,

"For the Spirit God gave us does not make us timid, but gives us power, love and self-discipline."

Perhaps if your own self-discipline is low, you need to ask God to change your timidity into His strength? What do you need His power to achieve in your life?

8. Lack of delegation

I used to struggle with this a great deal. Every year, for a long time, Jon and I led a team of young people to help run the 11-14's age group at a large Christian conference. It literally took me a whole year to plan it. I wrote outlines for every seminar (even ones that I wasn't leading). I minutely prepared every craft. I labelled every box. I felt I had to do it. But, years later, I realise that I could have done this so differently. I could have relied on the team to fulfil their potential more fully. This would have given them greater ownership, more opportunity to develop, and a greater sense of leadership. I think God has taken away some of that freakishly weird feeling that I need to micromanage others and I have learnt to work well as part of a team now. There is nothing more likely to stifle your own growth and the development of others than not delegating.

I take great comfort from the fact that Moses, the wonderful man who was the friend of God, also battled with the need to allocate responsibility. In Exodus 18 we see that Moses was wearing himself out being a judge for all the people's problems. Jethro, his father-in-law, questioned his actions:

"What you are doing is not good. You and these people who come to you will only wear yourselves out. The work is too heavy for you; you cannot handle it alone." (Exodus 18:13-24)

Do you notice anything that sounds familiar? Would anyone around you use similar words to describe your life right now?

Jethro went on to suggest that Moses select capable men and appoint them as officials to act as judges alongside him.

"'That will make your load lighter, because they will share it with you. If you do this and God so commands, you will be able to stand the strain, and all these people will go home satisfied.' Moses listened to his father-in-law and did everything he said."

It is easy to think that we have to be involved at every level of something we are engaged with. But it is also a lie. Finding capable people who can help us is vital if we are going to achieve all we need to do and take the time out that we need.

Perhaps you've read these last few pages feeling heavy and burdened by the weight of your current life patterns? Maybe you don't know how to change, or what you need to do in order to reset the balance and rest more fully? Have a look at these questions and pray that God will guide you through them as honestly as possible.

Rest Reflections:

- Do I celebrate my own exhaustion? Do I allow others to do so?
- What parts of my weekly, monthly or yearly schedule are toxic?
- Am I showing any signs of being spiritually undernourished? What can I do about this?
- Do I feel intimately connected to God at the moment? Why/ why not? What can I do to spend more time with Him?
- Where can I introduce space, calm and reflection to my day?
- Am I tired and lacking sleep? What can I do about this?
- Do I have a strong sense of fulfilling my own calling, or am I trying to do other people's jobs?
- Do I care for my physical body wisely, with good nutrition and exercise?
- What am I currently modelling to my partner/children/ friends about my work and rest?
- Am I a self-disciplined person? In what ways would greater discipline bless me?
- Do I suffer because I don't delegate tasks to others? What can I change in this area?

These are certainly challenging questions aren't they? As you reflect on them, you might like to read this wonderful piece by my friend Tina, to end this chapter.

Busy – by Tina Mann

Busyness used to be my trophy
I used to hold it up high
As I sank lower,
Crushed by its glory,
Drained of my power
But still it went higher
Look at my prize,
Look at my reward

Look at how happy I am when I can't sleep,
no time to eat,
mistreating my friends,
no time to extend mercy

Look at how I have no time to breathe,
suffocating as I gasp for some form of relief
Look at how much I am achieving,
filling my time so I don't have to stop

As if having no time was to be admired
As if being busy was to be applauded and cheered
Running, but the more I ran the more I ran out
The more I filled the more empty I became,
Nothing to pour out

So I'm chasing, running, mourning,
Caught in thoughts that were or could have been
I stay busy because then there is no time to be still

No time to consider the state of my heart and what is driving me
The motives for my actions
The reasons behind my trophy, my prize
So I keep preoccupied,
Scared of space and scared of time,
Of the things I would find if I was to stop and be still

I know I tried it
Took guts and courage to face this form of nothingness,
and this was new – I needed practise because what I found was
a whole load of restlessness,
some peace but mostly a mess
and a mind of busyness that did not want to stop.
My heart didn't stand a chance until my thinking calmed and
distractions faded
Being found by love in this moment of waiting
Focus on my breathing to ground me in this present moment

Because who can just be still
And that be enough?
Who can just stop and be at rest?
Without the haunts of yesterday taunting or the daunting
thoughts of tomorrow pulling forward my attention?
I faced what I feared when I stopped

This is my journey, my progress
Where my achievement was found in being
Where my success was doing nothing and being OK with it
This is where I can be met with perfect love, of just being enough
rather than doing enough

Busyness used to be my trophy
I used to hold it up high
But now I have no time for busyness
Because every second as it ticks by
Is full on its own
To be busy is an excuse and I now have no excuses.
Do you?

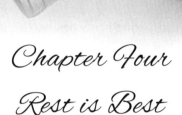

Chapter Four

Rest is Best

"Rest time is not wasted time. It is economy to gather fresh
strength. It is wisdom..."
– C.H. Spurgeon

Let go

When my children were younger, one of them was playing with
a box of bricks he'd got for his birthday. I was making a drink in
the kitchen when I heard him shouting "Lego!" repeatedly at the
top of his voice. I was pleased he was enjoying his gift. However,
when I went into the room, he was actually saying, "Let go!" to
one of his siblings, who was forcibly trying to take one of the
precious bricks from him.

Psalm 46:10a is an often-quoted verse of Scripture which
says, "Be still, and know that I am God."

This section of the verse appears on many Christian posters
depicting beautiful sunsets, fluffy kittens, running streams and
other peaceful scenes that don't bear much resemblance to
most people's day-to-day reality. But, did you know that the
phrase "Be still" in Hebrew actually means "Let go"? The Hebrew
definition is not so much about stopping, but more concerned
with surrendering.

When I was helping one of my younger brothers learn how to drive in an empty car park in Liverpool, there was a time when I actually had to "let go" of the steering wheel (which I had been surgically attached to for most of the first hour). I had to trust that he wouldn't ram the wall ahead. But I didn't let go until I was totally SURE he could drive straight AND find the brake!

In order to "let go" when we are trusting God with something, we need to be confident that He has got us and that He won't loosen His grip on us.

We are not very good at surrendering to God, are we? We often try and hold on very tightly to what He wants us to give back to Him. Perhaps that means our reputation, our finances, or our family. The act of surrender is a huge challenge in the midst of our hectic lives. We are surrounded by a society that tells us to look out for number one, be independent and work longer hours. But God asks us to surrender to Him, so that He can give us an exchange of His love and His peace.

For my 40th birthday I was given a handbag. It was a beautiful leather holdall, but I instantly knew I would never use it. It was too big for my body, a colour I don't wear and not really my style. I like patterns, bright colours, flowers, spots, anything that can induce a migraine. This bag was plain, brown leather and the size of a small field. So, I decided to see if I could take it back. I walked into Selfridges and semi-confidently asked the lady if she could organise an exchange for me.

She told me that the money would have to go on a store card. That was fine by me. Imagine my surprise when she handed me said card and a gift receipt with a value of £400 on it! I had NO idea what I was holding. This bag was an exclusive designer purchase. (I wouldn't know a designer bag if it bit me on the leg! I buy most of my clothes in charity shops and cheap stores). This bag was worth more than my first car. I stared at it as I handed it over. I knew it was expensive, but that didn't change the fact that I didn't need it and it didn't suit me. I had the best birthday treat ever, going around that store, buying lots of things that I really DID want. I felt truly RICH. And to me, of course, all of the items I gathered in my groaning basket were totally FREE. Hooray!

God has a wonderful habit of exchanging what we don't need and want for things we do. He exchanges our mourning for laughter, our loneliness for friendship, our hopelessness for expectant faith. We might not even deserve any of those things, but they are already paid for and dealt with. They are a free gift to us. What is more amazing, is that we get way beyond our expectations with God. We give Him one thing and He multiplies it into several things. God is the giver of good gifts. He never gives us something bad for us, or something that will ruin us. The Bible tells us in James 1:7 that, "every good and perfect gift" comes from God.

Recently, I was watching the ground-breaking BBC series *Blue Planet 2* about the deep oceans. The documentary suddenly showed a jellyfish-like creature that looked exactly like an umbrella. I shouted gleefully, "God invented umbrellas before we did!" at the screen. You see, every good idea that anyone has EVER had, was God's idea first. It mimics Him in some way.

There are some people who have the ability to give great presents, aren't there? You know, those who find you something you didn't know you needed, or didn't know was even a thing? And there are... well, other people who buy you something less personally relevant – and the only thing you can truthfully say is, "You really shouldn't have!" You say it again, "Oh, you really *shouldn't* have." And you truly mean it!

God is *never* like this. He is the ultimate present giver. But He gives us things our heart's need. He gives us rest when we are weary, sleep when we are aching, hope when we are despairing. He has always been a giver.

At the beginning of time, when there was nothing, He gave the world its form. He gave us seasons and sunshine. He gave us Venice and Venezuela. He gave us conifers and coal. Mountains and molecules. Panthers and parrots. He gave us each other. And more than all of this, much more, He gave us Himself in the person of Jesus. In the form of a homeless baby, born in a ramshackle shed to frightened, tired, young, poor, refugee parents.

It didn't look very promising. Most of the world totally MISSED it. But this one, unpromising act was the fulfilment of over 2,500 promises and prophecies.

God is not a convenience store kind of giver. He won't just give us what we ask for or what is on the prayer list. He's not a vending machine deity. He gives us what we need, yes. But so often, He gives us way MORE than we have asked for. The Bible says in Ephesians 3:20 that He gives us more than we can even ask or imagine. He gives us gifts that are "pressed down, shaken together and running over" as it says in Luke 6:38. He is a good Father who gives us what we need, what we don't deserve and what makes us experience life to the full. Why? Because He is our Dad.

What is it you need to let go of in order to receive something better from your heavenly Father?

Perhaps you need to let go of your fears, your stress, or your health worries? Maybe you need to surrender your job situation, who you will marry and where you will live? In my experience, whenever I have decided to give something to God, I have always received more back than I began with.

Perhaps one of the most important things we can ever give to the Lord is our tiredness. The Bible tells us that when we give that to Him, the exchange rate is extraordinary. It looks like this:

"But they who wait for the Lord shall renew their strength; they shall mount up with wings like eagles; they shall run and not be weary; they shall walk and not faint." (Isaiah 40:31)

Do you need a bit of that kind of supernatural energy? I know I do. The great preacher D.L. Moody was once asked, "Don't you get tired?" to which he replied, "I get tired *in* the work, but not tired *of* the work." God gives us His wonderful rest to help us carry on. So, what could that look like for you and what are the benefits of it?

What is rest?

John Mark Comer said,

"Sabbath is an expression of faith. Faith that there is a Creator and he's good. We are His creation. This is His world. We live under His roof, drink His water, eat His food, breathe His oxygen. So, on the Sabbath, we don't just take a day off from work; we take a day off from toil. We give Him all our fear and anxiety and stress and worry. We let go. We stop ruling and subduing, and we just be. We 'remember' our place in the universe. So that we never forget ... There is a God, and I'm not Him."

When I was asking the Lord about the rest in my life, I felt Him dropping all sorts of words into my heart. Funnily, they all begin with R! He pointed me to:

- Recreation
- Rebooting
- Relaxation
- Recovery
- Retreat
- Relationships

Let's take a look at what those might mean for us in the context of resting.

1. Recreation is defined as "an activity done for enjoyment when not working". But for me it is so much more than this. It is about allowing myself to be "re-created". The word comes from an older middle English one that means "mental or spiritual consolation". I love that definition. Many of us need to re-create ourselves. We need to re- create a sense of fun, enjoyment and play in our lives. We have become too boring, predictable and grown up. The cares of this life have absorbed us and robbed us of our childlikeness.

Occasionally, there are times when we say, mischievously, to our kids, "There are no grown-ups here. What shall we do?!" One day last week we all had a mad game of Hide and Seek, even though our eldest is now 13!

Winston Churchill thoroughly believed in the strength of hobbies and the power of play. But it was only at the age of 41, that he discovered one of his real passions. His sister-in-law, Lady Gwendoline Bertie (affectionately known as Goonie), first encouraged him to try painting. "Happy are the painters," Churchill later wrote, "for they shall never be lonely..."

It soon became an engrossing hobby that remained a large part of his life for the next 40 years.

Of painting he said, "I know nothing which, without exhausting the body, more entirely absorbs the mind." He also wrote, "When I get to heaven I mean to spend a considerable portion of my first million years in painting."

Erected in the 1930s, the studio at his home in Chartwell, in Westerham, Kent, became a special and favourite refuge for him. He was often found there and created over 500 paintings in his lifetime.

It is my theory that many of us carry at least one talent for something creative. It might be cooking, cross-stitch or calligraphy ... or ballet, book-binding or birdwatching. There will be something we are capable of that absorbs us and allows us deep, satisfying rest. If you don't know what your hobby is, perhaps it's time to do a bit of experimentation?

A few years back, during a period of grief following the death of some family members, I rather suddenly found myself totally immersed in the art of cake decorating. It utterly mesmerized me and I spent hours creating small world features for cakes for friends and family. I discovered great enjoyment in this pastime and I also found it a healing and captivating way to spend my time. If you had asked me 10 years before to make you a simple sponge cake, I would have been totally unable to do it. But slowly, with the help of books and online tutorials, I built up some skill, knowledge and experience. The happiness it gave me was heightened by the pleasure it gave others.

Another hobby I have is writing novels for my kids. None of them have ever been published, but I find them great fun to write and the kids adore being read a brand new chapter at night. The act of writing this kind of book relaxes me and often makes me laugh out loud.

What is it that you are yet to discover about yourself? What have you always longed to have a go at, but never allowed yourself time for? Perhaps this is the season for photography, whittling or floristry? Romans 12:6 says,

"In his grace, God has given us different gifts for doing certain things well."

What is your "certain thing"? Leo Buscaglia said, "Your talent is God's gift to you. What you do with it is your gift back to God." I hope this makes you think and gives you a nudge to just go for it!

What are the benefits of recreation?

As I have already said, I think our hobbies encourage us to feel a sense of playfulness and joy. Creating something new, whether it's a gourmet meal we've never made before, or a freshly-thrown clay masterpiece on a potter's wheel, can flood us with deep contentment.

I want to make a point here. Many people find resting, in the sense of doing nothing, unrelaxing because it can make them feel lethargic, lazy and low. Our activities can help us take a purposeful break from work, but still give us a much-needed sense of achievement.

Sometimes our hobbies introduce us to new people or new places which, in itself, can be an outlet for stress. The novel challenges and fresh knowledge we gain from learning a different skill can be invigorating.

Hobbies can also help us to stay mindful. We can't be absorbed by something fully and be dwelling on the past or on a problem. A deep activity helps us be in that moment and that moment only. Research has also shown that certain hobbies can even help us stay well. Having fun is associated with healthy blood pressure and will even lower levels of depression. The third

President of the United States, Thomas Jefferson, wrote, "It is neither wealth not splendour, but tranquility and occupation which gives happiness."

It is worth saying that when we are creating something, we are obviously copying God, from whom all our creativity ultimately comes. When God made us in His image, He made us not just capable of creation, but to crave it. He gave us the gene, the DNA and the desire to make things beautiful. For some, this might be designing a relaxing home environment, or a useful spreadsheet, or an item of clothing. We are all so different, but each of us reflects the creative character of God.

Gertrud Mueller Nelson wrote, "When we are creative, we are most like God. When we take something that is formless and make something of it, when we give the untamed and unbounded a shape, a name and a meaning, we are creating and communicating with the transcendent."

2. Rebooting. I agree with John Mark Comer who wrote in his book, *Garden City: Work, Rest and the Art of Being Human*, "We need to relearn how to power down, unplug, disconnect, take a break, and be in one place at one time. We forget that we're not a machine. We can't work 24/7."

In Mark 6:31, we see that Jesus said,

"Come with me by yourselves to a quiet place and get some rest."

We all need time to switch off, reboot and regain energy. We see regularly throughout the gospels that Jesus went off by Himself in order to recharge. Luke 5:16 (NIV) tells us,

"But Jesus often withdrew to lonely places and prayed."

This is interesting to me. Jesus knew that He needed time alone with God. He knew He had to take Himself away from others to "lonely places" in order to do that. Do we copy that example or do we constantly surround ourselves with noise and busyness?

Why do we need to reboot a computer? I am no technical expert, but I know that when a computer has too many tasks to run, or a set of physical events occur in a sequence that the software programmers just weren't expecting, then the computer's activities can get "stuck". We are the same. Sometimes we reach an impasse. We just need to start again, to switch off for a while. Reboots do not work if you switch the appliance that has ceased to function straight back on. You have to wait a while.

During the writing of this book I have been experimenting with a number of rebooting activities to see what difference it has made to my day.

I have gone out for coffee with friends instead of working all day.

I have limited the hours at my desk to less than half my usual time spent.

I have been to the cinema during the daytime (I know! How decadent!)

I have completely separated myself from my phone for long periods during the day.

I have switched off my Instagram account.

I have seen a personal trainer.

I have begun doing some abstract oil painting.

I have made new recipes we have never eaten before.

I have listened to new podcasts.

I have experimented with new music to listen to.

I am not going to lie to you, at first some of these things felt alarming. This book has not progressed nearly as fast as other ones I have penned. Sometimes I have found that frustrating and have been tempted to worry that it won't hit the deadline. But then I felt an exchange of emotions as I realised afresh that God was in charge of the writing process, not me. I have felt this to be a much more creative, fun and free time in my life.

A few months back when I turned off Instagram, it felt odd. I ceased to know what my friends and family were up to in such detail. But, as the weeks have progressed, I have discovered it to be very freeing. I have felt less time pressure, less comparison in my heart and less frenzy in my spirit. I know I will use it quite differently, and much more sparingly, if ever I do turn it on again. Another result of this has been a closer connection to my family. My husband, brothers, their wives and my Dad and his wife are all on a Whatsapp group together. I have noticed that this has steadily become more used by us all as a family over the past few months. Is that connected to me having less time on other forms of social media? I am not sure. But it has been a lovely bonus.

Mark Buchanan said, "Most of the things we need to be most fully alive never come in busyness. They grow in rest."

Is there anything you need to do to exercise a kind of reboot in your own life?

3. Relaxation. As a small child, my mother bought us *The Wind in The Willows* on audio tape. We listened to the story very often. It is a book that made a huge impression on me. One of my favourite quotes from its pages is made about Mole, who decides to leave his spring cleaning and whitewashing and go for a walk. He gets great joy from being "out" when other creatures are "in". Author Kenneth Grahame writes, "After all, the best part of a holiday is perhaps not so much to be resting yourself, as to see all the other fellows busy working." There is something powerful and wonderful about having a day off when everyone else is "on". But this takes discipline. If you like, it means we need to "put on fresh eyes". It means we need to reframe our lives and realise our need for refreshing and relaxing.

I was incredibly blessed this week to get to sing a timely song by a great friend of ours. The song is called *Pause* by Andy Smith. I think it sums up what difference stillness with God makes.

Pause – be still and know
Put on fresh eyes
And see that He is God

Wait – wait for the Lord
Strengthen your heart
And know that He will come

Still waters – comfort my soul
Your hands – scatter the shadows

Woah, nothing greater than
Woah, nothing sweeter than your love
Nothing greater than your love for us

Rest – lean on His heart
There is no striving
When you know that you're loved

You build a house
Made from Your presence
It is my home
Your loving kindness

There is a table
Full of your blessing
There is no ceiling
There I see heaven!

I wish you could hear this song. It's stunning! I love those precious words and I am praying them now as a prayer over you, as you read them. Perhaps you need to rest and "lean on His heart".

Relaxation is good for us. It is clinically proven to protect our physical hearts and our bodies. High levels of stress can mean we suffer from poor heart health – high blood pressure, palpitations and hypertension. There are also many studies that show how stress is comparable to other risk factors like a poor diet or lack of exercise (according to Kathi Heffner Ph.D, assistant professor of psychiatry at the Rochester Centre for Mind-Body Research, New York). But relaxing lowers our risk factors. It even lessens the likelihood of catching colds. It is known to boost our brain power and enhance memory. It helps us stay calm, make better life decisions and be less self-absorbed.

A recent BBC article by Health and Science reporter, James Gallagher confirmed that Public Health England (PHE) considered that 1/5 of all patient antibiotics were unnecessarily prescribed. The headline was, "Patients need rest not antibiotics says Health official."

Relaxing also protects the spiritual heart. The Bible tells us that our hearts are the wellspring of life. Proverbs 4:23 says,

"Guard your heart more than anything else, because the source of your life flows from it."

I think some of us are very poor at spending time focusing on our own needs. Asking questions like, "How do I feel? What is going well for me? What do I need to change?" can make the difference between being ill or being well. Scientists who study our thoughts and our brains now think that we have more than 50,000 separate thoughts every single day! What do you think I would find if I just flipped your brain open and examined yours? How many of those thoughts of yours would be positive, restful ones? How many would bring you blessing and peace?

If our hearts and minds are sick, we can't cope with anything. If our hearts are anxious we feel fearful and isolated. Maybe you need to check your heart today and see how you are feeling?

4. Recovery. Over the years I have met many people in "recovery". This might be from an illness, operation or addiction. We go through a great deal as humans and our minds and bodies need time to mend. (I talk a lot about addiction recovery in my book *The Habit Breaker – how to change for good*). Health and fitness trainers tell us that rest is just as important for muscle growth as repetitions (lifting weights or continuing an exercise). If we overtrain or work our bodies too hard we will see a decrease in our energy, a lowering of performance, and even a dip in our immunity. We may even experience pain, disturbed sleep and greater levels of tension. Any physical exercise we do, from weights to interval training, will damage and tear our muscle fibres. But during rest our muscles can reconstruct or recover in stronger formations and increased size.

There is also a need to recover spiritually from the emotional barrages we face each week. I know that if I don't rest well after I have given out a large amount, I will be tired, grumpy and unable to function at my heart's best for myself and my family. For example, my part-time job as a School Listener can sometimes be quite sad. I often get to hear stories of children, young people and adults who have experienced great trauma or hardship. I MUST rest well from my work days in order to make sure I am wise next time. I cannot afford to go into that tiny room feeling tired, cynical or far from God. I am desperate for His help, presence and assurance as I listen and speak to the precious people trusting me with their heavy loads.

I don't know what you do for work, or what stresses you are currently under, but I know you need time to recover. During the Second World War, the heads of the Enigma section at Bletchley Park made sure that a chess board was always nearby for their workers. For people of their brain capacity, the game was effortlessly absorbing, but also allowed their minds some recovery from the brutal, high-level work required of them.

What do you need in order to recover at the moment?

It might be helpful for you to write down ways in which you gain energy and make sure you action those things each week. I have to go for a walk every weekday. I need fresh air, exercise and the perspective of getting out to keep my mood buoyant.

I also need detachment activities – things that have nothing to do with my work – like cooking, exercising and meeting friends. I have to feel disconnected from my jobs to help me recover more quickly.

German Sociologist Sabine Sonnentag explored what provides the best kinds of recovery. Her findings were that, "Workers who have the chance to get away mentally, switch off and devote their energies elsewhere, are more productive, have better attitudes, get along better with their colleagues and are better able to deal with challenges at work."

How are you feeling right now? Do you need to have more detachment from the things that are causing you stress and anxiety? How can you help that to happen? Joshua 1:9 (ESV) says,

> "Have I not commanded you? Be strong and courageous. Do not be frightened, and do not be dismayed, for the Lord your God is with you wherever you go."

5. Retreat. I love going away on retreat. I find it recalibrates my heart and helps me function well to have deep time out, away from my friends, family and "normal" life.

When I am on retreat, I don't like speaking to people. This surprises some. Because I am such a sociable person, most people think I like to be chatty all the time. Far from it! When on retreat, I try to maintain what I call a "gentle silence". I won't be rude or offhand to anyone, but my heart is that I remain open to the things God might want to say to me. I have such little silence in my life that I crave it in my retreat times. I have had to stop going to certain retreat places because there is too much noise there for me.

Some people can find silence an intimidating thing. They associate it with negatives. But I have found, for myself, that being still and silent can help me to address issues that have been bothering me in busyness. It doesn't take me long to find answers in quietness.

If we aren't careful we can overfill our lives. All too readily, our days can become one long wave of work, internet surfing, TV watching, eating, and juggling the demands of our families and friends. It can sometimes feel as though we never have any space at all. None of these activities are bad in themselves.

However, if they are used to fill a vacuum that is not being filled, over time, that pattern will manifest itself in some way.

Just today I read that a former Facebook employee has written his concerns about the result of using social media as much as we do. Chamath Palihapitiya, who joined Facebook as an executive in 2007, accused his old employer in particular of "programming" its users and said he no longer uses the website or allows his children to access it. He wrote,

> "We curate our lives around this perceived sense of perfection because we get rewarded in these short-term signals, hearts and likes and thumbs up. We conflate that with value and we conflate that with truth, and instead what it really is – fake, brittle popularity that's short term and leaves you even more vacant and empty."

I have written many times about my concerns regarding Facebook and other social media platforms, so I won't add any more here. I just believe that there are many things that take up our time, but don't add great value to our lives. Perhaps one benefit of reading this book is that it will help to challenge you about your own online habits and patterns? What I would love is that we each keep a check on our hearts, that we are not wasting our days doing things that create lost relationships, lost opportunities and lost dreams.

Sometimes it can feel as though life is really coming at us. Everything feels like it is going wrong. Psalm 3:1-6 (TLB) speaks of this feeling, saying,

> "I have so many enemies. So many say that God will never help me. But Lord, you are my shield, my glory, and my only hope. You alone can lift my head, now bowed in shame.

I cried out to the Lord, and he heard me from his Temple in Jerusalem. Then I lay down and slept in peace and woke up safely, for the Lord was watching over me. And now, although ten thousand enemies surround me on every side, I am not afraid."

For me, this is the joyful perspective God gives us when we go away and spend time on our own with Him.

The ability to gain meaningful and extended detachment from normal life is something many well-known business people subscribe to. For example, Bill Gates takes what he calls regular "Think weeks". These are not retreats from work, but rather times away from his usual workload and colleagues. His cabin for this purpose is only accessible by seaplane and has no room for family or assistants. Except for a cook, who brings him two meals a day, he doesn't see anyone during these times – not even his wife. He sleeps in a small bedroom that takes up a corner of the cottage and spends all day reading and taking notes. This practice has begun to be copied by other business leaders as they have seen how effective Bill's mind and business practices are following these retreats.

6. Relationships. Each of us needs at least some rest in the context of relationship. Bill Johnson said, "It's brilliant to recognize that we need other people to complete what we carry." Now, for some of us, that presents a real challenge. One of my friends was chatting to me about this a few weeks ago. She is a beautiful girl who has not yet met the person of her dreams. She asked me the tough question, "OK, so how do you expect me to do this? How can I rest with others? I get home and I am alone. Does the Telly count?!"

Let me explain more of what I mean. We all know that it is possible to be surrounded by people but feel lonely. It is also possible to be alone, but not feel in any way isolated or unhappy. I mean something more profound than this.

I think God designed us *out of* community (He is a trinity – a group of 3) *for* community. This means that some aspects of ourselves will only be truly at home and find their best expression when we are with other people who love us. But this doesn't mean ALL the time. We have already spoken about how Jesus went off by Himself to solitary places to be alone, to gather strength and to pray. But we also see Him partying with friends, hanging out in people's homes, on mountains, beaches and in town squares. We all need EVENT-based rest. That will look different for each of us. Not all of us crave going out for a drink in a noisy bar with 10 mates. But some of us really do. We LOVE that environment and thrive in it and seek it. For others, we need a beach BBQ or a firepit in a garden to help us unwind, make sense of ourselves, and feel a deep peace again. In our busy schedules those things need diary dates attached.

There are 6 of us in our family, so there are many things to be considered. Piano lessons, work commitments, Grow Group, church, Youth night, gymnastics, friends, family. It is a familiar pattern. If I am not careful I can get to the end of a week and realise that I have not had any time to chat deeply to Jon, or to my best friends.

I can't live like that for long without becoming a bit resentful. If I don't watch it, I can start to take my busyness out on others when it's actually MY fault. Maybe you know what that's like? The older I get the more I say to people, "Can we put a date in?" It sounds terribly grown up, but it seems to be the only way that I can get to see people who help me rest and recover and understand what God is doing in me.

Elisabeth Elliot wrote, "Work is a blessing. God has so arranged the world that work is necessary, and He gives us hands and strength to do it. The enjoyment of leisure would be nothing if we had only leisure. It is the joy of work well done that enables us to enjoy rest, just as it is the experiences of hunger and thirst that make food and drink such pleasures."

Rest Reflections:

- Am I inhibited by my own busyness? In what ways can I see this impacting my life?
- What practical steps can I take today to restore some recreation and play in my life?
- Do I have a hobby or activity that satisfies me and helps me rest?
- When was the last time I took time out or went on a retreat? Do I need to book one?
- Who do I need to be more intentional about seeing regularly?
- What event-based rest do I need? What can I do to help that happen soon?

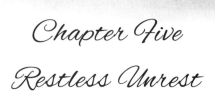

Chapter Five

Restless Unrest

"Advice for discouraged sailors:
Stop.
Steady your boat.
Study your compass.
Seek the wind."
– Brad Montague

Time poverty

You might argue with me, as some people have, that you don't have TIME to rest. Your life is too busy. The demands on you are too high. The work is too hard. Your kids are too needy. You get little sleep because you have a small baby. Or you work shifts. I hear you. I really do. But the plain truth is that you have just as many minutes in your day as everyone else. The focus for you is on what you are choosing to DO with that precious commodity. I can promise you (from personal, hard-fought experience) that there are many different ways to rest, even as a busy parent, or a newly-qualified teacher. But it can certainly feel like a battle to get the relaxation we need. It can be *hard work* not to work too hard, can't it?

Part of the reason for this is that our enemy loves to keep us busy and unable to rest. He knows that a tired person is less likely to be wise, discerning or thoughtful in their decision making. He understands that rest is the atmosphere that faith thrives in. So, he takes great delight in sowing untruths to us about us relaxing. As I alluded to in the introduction, there are some lies that he whispers into our minds:

- You can't afford to take time off!
- You have too much to do!
- No one else can do this job like you!
- If you don't do this now, something bad will happen!
- You can't do this another time! It has to be done today/now.

Are any of those statements familiar to you? Do they find a way to keep seeping into your own consciousness? I know that even today, a number of them have found their way into my head! Busyness like this taps into our ego. It makes us feel vitally important, needed and active. So, we choose to believe the propaganda and keep striving, even if we are shattered and in dire need of a lengthy lie down!

The problem many of us find is this: the challenges we face are so unique to the generation we're a part of that we are still working out how to combat them. Let's take a look at some of those issues.

Tightening the Commuter Belt
Years ago, people worked where they lived, sometimes quite literally in their own homes, or nearby. Now, we are much more divorced from our surroundings, often leaving early in the morning and only returning to our homes late at night.

According to research by the Trades Union Congress (TUC) in

the UK, the number of people spending more than two hours travelling to and from work every day has jumped by 72% in the past decade. That's two hours a day effectively not at home or at work! Time in a kind of limbo land. A 2011 census even showed that 100 people a week commute from the Orkney Islands (which for those of you who don't know, are above mainland Scotland) to Southwark in South London, which is a journey covering an eye-wateringly lengthy 530 miles. This begs the question "Why?!" Especially when you consider that the commute involves at least two plane flights and costs several hundred pounds. I wonder if anyone in those 100 people's lives has been tempted to whisper the words, "Move house" to their pals? I know I would!

Our journey times are getting longer as the amount of people travelling increases. Pollution, congestion and cities in need of constant regeneration all add to the mix. The heightened stress caused by the lack of control we experience when travelling, added to the potential of delays, boredom, isolation or unpleasant journeys due to the behaviour, closeness or attitude of others, can cause lower life satisfaction and increase anxiety. In fact, statistics show that personal happiness decreases with every mile a commuter travels. A study in 2014 showed that the average New York taxi travels at 8.5 mph and it won't be a relaxing ride. When I was in a taxi in Brooklyn last year, travelling to the airport, the driver used his horn about 35 times in the hour-long, stop/start journey. Bangkok traffic in rush hour reaches the heady heights of 7mph. Mexico, the world's most congested city, is buried under a fog of smog. And, of course, all of this can contribute to our lack of rest.

What is the answer?

In all honesty, I think some of us need to take a hard look at

WHY we are working so hard, choosing to live where we do, or spending so much time away from our home environments. It is all too easy to find ourselves "keeping up with the Jones's", when perhaps they are trying to do the same thing with you. Promotion at work, or the offer of more responsibility, feels like something an ambitious, career-minded worker should head towards. But what if that ambition is directly opposed to spending time with your wife/husband and kids? What if that job means more travel abroad, less time off and less free time at weekends? Family goals matter just as much, if not MORE than the career-centred ones. Yet sometimes they don't seem to get as much traction. Someone once said that the darkest place in a lighthouse is the base. This can sadly be true for the family too. We can spend so long radiating all our light and energy to the world around us, that our families don't get a look in.

I don't know your domestic situation. You may be single, married, divorced, living with a partner or bereaved. But I do know that family life is one of God's greatest priorities for us. Psalm 128:3-4 (ESV) says,

"Your wife will be like a fruitful vine within your house; your children will be like olive shoots around your table. Yes, this will be the blessing for the man who fears the Lord."

You might not have 2.4 kids and a surburban semi, but there will be people in your life who are significant to you. Are they getting enough of your time and resources?

Sir Tom Farmer, a UK business man and CEO of a large motor company said, "Too often those of us heavily involved in the business world are in danger of losing out on our most important asset – our family."

Is that how your family feel to you? Your "most important asset"? Or are they a group of people you feel you are letting down right now?

When life is busy, it can feel as though the people who matter to us most are the ones who get squeezed out.

I recently read about a Canadian businessman who refused to believe he could take a lower paid job because of all his financial commitments – one of which was an expensive cabin in the woods. The cabin was a 3-hour drive away. When he and the family got there after bad traffic on a Friday, it was always after dark. He would wake up on Saturday and the cabin would invariably need some repairs or chores doing around it. The family would spend time apart as he worked on the cabin. Then they would leave early on Sunday to avoid the traffic again.

Does that cabin sound like a dream investment to you?

Maybe it did, at first. Perhaps it was the temptation of lazy Sundays by the lake that first persuaded the man to purchase it. But now?

Are we in danger of being like this man? Working hard for a lifestyle that doesn't live up to the promise we bought into? Can we be like this with people too? I know that I can have good intentions about spending family time at weekends which all too readily gets swamped by that extra church activity, a person needing me, or that work project. Maybe there are close relationships in our lives that need more of our thinking. Pastor Wayne Cordeiro said,

> "Your marriage, which early on seemed to maintain itself, will no longer survive the way it used to. Healthy marriages require intentionality and planned investment. So will your waistline, your family, your ministry, your faith and your emotional health."

We all need to be wise enough to ask ourselves some tough questions. "What am I giving my life to? What am I striving to achieve? And, critically, is it WORTH it? It is possible to be totally blinded by something and not know it. Recently, I read about a 67-year-old lady who went into hospital for routine cataract surgery. During the operation, surgeons removed 27 contact lenses from her eye. Seventeen of those had fused together to form one blue mass. The other 10 were recovered from other places in her eye. Astonishingly the patient had not complained of any irritation.

Is there something you are blind to right now? Perhaps you need to pray, ask your family and friends and get their perspectives too. Jeremiah 6:16 (NKJV) helps us here. It says,

> "Thus says the Lord,
> 'Stand in the ways and see,
> And ask for the old paths, where the good way is,
> And walk in it;
> Then you will rest for your souls.'"

We are always attracted by new shiny things. But this passage endorses the "old paths" – the familiar things we already know. Winston Churchill said,

> "There is no doubt that it is around the family and the home that all the greatest virtues, the most dominating virtues of human society, are created, strengthened and maintained."

Do your family goals need a little work? Churchill's words here are very wise. We need time to create, strengthen and maintain our time with those dearest to us.

Overworked

It is no surprise to you, I'm sure, that our working weeks are getting longer. According to the Education Policy Institute, most full time teachers work an average of 48.2 hours per week. But, one in five teachers works 60 hours or more – 12 hours over the limit set by the European working time directive. Teacher retention in schools is also a huge problem as teachers work too hard, for too long and then burn out. The NHS is also under pressure as more medical staff cite long hours with less breaks as the reason for them leaving the system. Many other services and sectors say the same.

The Shops Act of 1950 prohibited shops opening and trading on a Sunday. When I was little, if we ran out of bread on that day, we did without. But doing without is unheard of in our "have it now" generation. Back in 1994, a change in Sunday trading laws meant that shops had the ability to open every day. Once one shop could open, they all had to. Now we can buy anything we like on a Sunday – from a harpoon to a herringbone tweed cap – albeit within slightly more restricted hours. I think this is such a shame. We have given people an expectation that we want them to work on a day when they could be resting and being with their families.

And actually, our long hours have not resulted in greater productivity. They have not rescued our failing economy or provided better pay or job security. Long hours only show people that we are serious, hard-working and tired, not that we are producing better work. I am sure you will have had a day when you worked for too long and ended up having to redo the work you did, because of its poor quality. In today's open plan office world, leaders may scan the floor for who "looks busy", but this is often a poor marker for productivity or creative flow.

We can find ourselves staying later at the office because it is "expected" of us. Our job description may declare that our hours and responsibilities are one thing, but our bosses may appear to demand more. No one wants to be the first person to go home, as it looks like they are lazier than others. It takes real strength to discipline ourselves in this area and grab our coats at 5.30pm.

Overtime
Many of us are willing to work overtime for more pay. But, a piece of (somewhat unlikely) research done by the International Gamers Development Association found that personal productivity drops immediately when a person starts working overtime. Amazingly, the research showed that the total work done in 60 hours was the same as that which would have been achieved in a 40-hour week. In other words, 20 hours were TOTALLY wasted, achieving very little! The study also stated that, "In the short term, working over 21 hours continuously is equivalent to being 'legally drunk'." How crazy is that? Longer periods of continuous work were also shown to drastically reduce cognitive function and increase the chance of catastrophic error. The study also found that in both the short and long-term, reducing sleep hours as little as one hour nightly can result in a severe decrease in cognitive ability, sometimes without workers perceiving that there is any problem.

It is true that "tiredness kills".

Does this all sound a bit familiar? Have you found yourself a victim of that kind of rat-race lifestyle? Are you surrounded by tired, stressed, frazzled colleagues whose mental and physical health is worrying you? Even in churches we can wear busyness as some sort of badge of honour, as though it pleases God.

During my study for this book, I discovered that the term

"workaholic" was first coined in a study of ministers. How sad is that? It is very possible to wear ourselves out working FOR God, forgetting that we should be working WITH HIM. Some statistics from the Duke Divinity School's clergy health initiative in the US found that 25% – one quarter of their full-time pastors – were suffering from emotional exhaustion, de-personalisation (the feeling of a lack of control and watching your life from a sense of distance) and a reduced sense of accomplishment. These are three markers of burnout which regularly lead to poorer health and higher than average rates of obesity, illness, depression and anxiety.

But the Bible has a wonderful solution to our frenzy. Matthew 11:28 (ESV) clearly says,

"Come to me, all who labour and are heavy laden, and I will give you rest."

Doesn't that phrase just fill you with hope?

I love it!

Perhaps some of us, and some of our leaders, have forgotten how to "Come to the Lord"? We need to let go of the illusion that we are indispensable to the running of the cosmos.

At University, my prayer partner was a very godly girl called Rosie. I remember when life went wrong or things looked impossible, she would quote her Dad, Sandy, who apparently often said, "The Lord reigns." No doubt, no fear, no "power of hell or scheme of man" can come against that eternal truth. We all need times where we *re*-recognise that God is on the throne.

Staycation

There are some nations who are statistically very good at

holidaying. If you have ever been in Paris over the summer you will know that, like many European cities, many Parisian workers clear out during the month of August as they all go away on annual leave. In fact, according to a new study from Expedia, French workers take 30 full days off – equivalent to a whole month each year. The same study found that people in Japan take the least amount of vacation days per year. Statistics show that they only take 5 on average. FIVE days off in 365 days! That is painful, isn't it?!

People who choose not to go on holidays might feel they are saving themselves money, but they will cost their companies and themselves more in terms of illness, burnout and emotional exhaustion.

The phrase "I need a holiday!" has never been more apt.

In the Old Testament in Esther 9:20-22 we read,

"Mordecai recorded these things and sent letters to all the Jews who were in all the provinces of King Ahasuerus, both near and far, obliging them to keep the fourteenth day of the month Adar and also the fifteenth day of the same, year by year, as the days on which the Jews got relief from their enemies, and as the month that had been turned for them from sorrow into gladness and from mourning into a holiday; that they should make them days of feasting and gladness, days for sending gifts of food to one another and gifts to the poor."

Even thousands of years ago, four centuries before Jesus, the Jews recognised their need for holiday, feasting and fun. This time was set apart for gladness and partying, as well as giving to others and to the poor. Many of us need to have more deliberate markers in the diary like this.

When was the last time you had a decent amount of time off? Time away from your phone, your laptop, your schedule and all the big and little the demands on your time? When did you last put an "out of office" notice on your email?

If you can't remember, or you had to qualify the answer in some way, perhaps God might be challenging you.

Psalm 127: 2 (AMP) says:

"It is vain for you to rise early,
To retire late,
To eat the bread of anxious labours –
For He gives [blessings] to His beloved even in his sleep."

Breakdown in community

The tragically murdered British MP Jo Cox identified loneliness as a serious problem in her constituency. She saw it damaging the wealth, health and wellbeing of people of all ages, and set out to investigate what could be done in her community to strengthen social ties. In her memory, colleagues have continued to look at the issues around social isolation and "The Jo Cox Commission on Loneliness" contains fascinating but heart-rending statistics.

Amongst the findings were that one in four parents felt cut off from friends and support and that being isolated is as bad for people as smoking 15 cigarettes a day.

It is true to say that in many places our community ties are weaker than ever. Families are broken apart through relationship problems. People no longer know their neighbours. Social mobility, migration and the refugee crisis, together with the state of the global job market, means that people in the same family network can now live thousands of miles apart. The impact of this on society and our rest time in particular is dramatic. People are not able to share workloads and the responsibilities of caring for children or the elderly. Loneliness across multi-generations is rife and mental health stresses are huge. Many people can feel isolated, anxious and forgotten.

The wonderful truth is that the Church is the best kind of family in the world! Wherever Christians get together, there is a family reunion. We can share with people of different ages and backgrounds and celebrate life together. We can support those in fear, debt and worry. We can rejoice with those who rejoice and mourn with those who mourn (Romans 12:15). As a family, we genuinely could not survive without our church network. We love them and know that they love us.

Psalm 68:6 (NLT) says, "God places the lonely in families; he sets the prisoners free and gives them joy."

In the last few months I have found this verse to be especially poignant. I realised that I wanted to do something myself about the loneliness of elderly people in my area. But in truth, I felt overwhelmed by the scale of the problem. Paralysed by the government statistics, I was unsure where to turn to offer my help. I was also aware of the limits on my time. A God-encounter in the street led me to stumble across a small charity in Manchester who befriend the elderly. I contacted them, was given training and then was matched (very carefully) to a lady who is house-bound. She was a prisoner in her own home. Aside from her carers, who get her dressed and feed her, this person regularly had no visitors and no one to talk to face-to-face ALL week.

When I started seeing her, the difference it made was incredible. She told me that I had brought joy into her life (remember that verse from Psalm 68?). She has said at various times that her legs feel stronger and her health improves when

I see her. But the amazing thing is, I am not sure who enjoys our time more! I get a huge boost from visiting this intelligent woman who was once a teacher in the armed forces in Germany. Her life story is unrelentingly interesting, her quiet conversation is exciting and her company is gently absorbing.

Now, you may think, what has looking after a house-bound elderly person got to do with a book on rest?

Let me share what I have found.

Years ago, I went on a holiday with my family on the River Thames in a canal barge. At first, I found the 4mph pace of our boat annoyingly slow. I just wanted us to GET somewhere quicker than we were. The buzzing chaos of my brain did not delight in the gentle slowness of canal living. But I soon relished the ability to be going at a speed that enabled me to enjoy every vista on the journey. In almost every other way I had ever travelled, scenes had zipped past my eyes at a rate of knots. But on a narrow boat, time slipped sideways. I needed that holiday to help me stop.

We all benefit from people who allow us the chance to calm down and enjoy what we have. Visiting this precious lady physically slows my heart rate (I have one of those clever watches that tells me my pulse and so this is totally true). I stop and relax completely. She becomes my only focus. I truly rest in her presence.

This lady and I have done one another the power of good. Gently, we have encouraged one another in different areas. Some weeks I have taken her something I have baked from a cook book she gave me. I am delighted to say that the NHS have given us a wheelchair and we are looking forward to some trips out of the house soon.

But they will be at a very slow pace!

Who can you spend time with who allows you to take a breath and come to a standstill? Who could encourage your heart rate to slow and your perspective to shift?

Goal shift

Humans have always wanted success. But I believe that our goals and goal posts have changed considerably in my lifetime. Years ago, people wanted monetary security and a decent roof over their heads. Today we're more focused than ever on personal fame, image, possessions and status than ever before. Academic authors like Dr Tim Kasser have correlated these shifting goals to an increase in both anxiety and depression.

The young people I chat to each week see the fatuous, futile lives of certain celebrities and, for reasons beyond my understanding, want to emulate them. They are obsessed with their own personal appearance, believing their teeth aren't white enough, their waistlines aren't thin enough and their hair isn't shiny enough.

And that's just the boys.

I would love to see them attaching credence to more REAL heroes in the world. I try and point out to them those people whose lives are purposeful and whose existences point to something more virtuous and everlasting.

There has never been more need for the truth of the Gospel and the community of the Church! We have SUCH good news to share and we need to be bold in declaring it. I love the potency of these words from Isaiah 40:7-9 (NIV):

"Surely the people are grass.
The grass withers and the flowers fall,
but the word of our God endures forever.

You who bring good news to Zion,
go up on a high mountain.
You who bring good news to Jerusalem,
lift up your voice with a shout,
lift it up, do not be afraid;
say to the towns of Judah,
'Here is your God!'"

Every fad will fade. Every new thing will die out. But God's Word and His truth never will. We can rest assured of that.

Lack of peace
John MacArthur wrote,

"Some people cannot rest mentally and emotionally because they are so easily annoyed. Every little nuisance upsets them and they always feel hassled. Rest does not mean freedom from all nuisances and hassles; it means freedom from being so easily bothered by them."

A few months ago, I was in Leicester to see a theatre show with the family. On the way, we were alarmed by an altercation between two men whilst we were crossing a main road. One of the men leapt into the street before the light turned green causing the second man behind him to exclaim.

The first man turned around (in the middle of the road) and aggressively raising his voice said, "What did you say?"

Man 2 stuttered, "I..I..I thought you were going to be hurt. I didn't think it had gone green yet."

"Mind you own (insert swearword) business!" shouted Man 1 angrily. He then swore again before storming off.

So much anger for so little reason! Why is it that we have so much road rage, anger management and stress-related anxiety? Why does every programme on iPlayer come with a warning that it "Contains strong language"? Perhaps like me, you long for the day when you read that a programme, "Contains gentle language and monks doing a wordsearch."

But I am realistic. Our programmes only accurately reflect our culture. We expect strong language on the TV because we are surrounded by it on the bus.

Many of us need to take time out to re-establish some balance. Aren't you glad that God describes himself as "slow to anger and abounding in love?" (Psalm 103:8)

What about you?

Do you find yourself easily wound up? Are you someone who takes offence easily?

Are your stress levels so high that you get angry if you're in a queue of one? Ralph Waldo Emerson said, "For every minute you remain angry, you give up sixty seconds of peace of mind."

Take my advice and take some time out. Seek God and ask Him to reveal the source of your stress to you. It could be that you have not taken proper care of yourself for many years.

Lack of sleep

More of us struggle to sleep than ever before. We are a tired generation, but some of us seem unable to catch up on the rest our bodies need. So, why is this the case?

Amongst the reasons health experts cite are:

A) An increase in people taking medications or drugs that disturb sleep
B) People drinking more caffeine

C) Higher alcohol consumption. While alcohol is well known to help you fall asleep quickly, too much can disrupt sleep in the second half of the night as the body begins to process the alcohol.

D) Depression or anxiety

E) Snoring due to greater obesity levels

F) Shift work

G) An increase in screen time, which damages our sleep hormones

H) Stressful events

I) Jet lag

This all sounds pretty depressing, doesn't it? But the good news is that God has given us a wonderful antidote to our lack of rest. The Bible tells us that He gives His beloved sleep (Psalm 127:2).

Are you His beloved?

Yes?

Then you need not fear. Sleep is yours! But there are some practical things we can do to help us sleep better. If you are struggling to get a good night, there are a number of suggested solutions you can try:

PRAY: Prayer helps turn our stresses over to God. It encourages us to remember His sovereignty. It opens us up to the assets and answers of Heaven. It reminds us we are loved and chosen.

EXERCISE: Many experts agree that exercise is the number one factor that will help promote good sleep. Apparently as little as 10 minutes of aerobic exercise, such as walking or cycling, can drastically improve the quality and quota of our sleep.

EATING SLEEP FRIENDLY FOODS: Steering clear of heavy, rich or fried food which may trigger indigestion for some people can also be helpful.

LIGHT: Getting enough natural light during the day is also important. Exposure to sunlight during the day, and maintaining darkness at night helps to maintain a healthy circadian rhythm cycle. Consider using blackout curtains or an eye mask to make it as dark as possible.

BEDTIME ROUTINE: Having a regular nightly routine helps the body recognise when it is time to switch off. Things like taking a warm bath, reading a book or listening to quiet music are all known to help.

MAKE NOTES: Sometimes when we get into bed, we can find our brains whizz and whirr with all that we need to do the next day. It can help to have a pen and paper handy, just to note down anything you don't want to forget.

BLUE LIGHT: Bright blue light from lamps, mobiles, laptops and TV screens can make it difficult to fall asleep, and can cause sleep disturbance. The advice is to so turn those lights off or adjust them when possible an hour before bed.

SOUNDS: Many people like some gentle noise when they fall asleep. There are "white noise" machines, humidifiers, fans and other devices that can make the bedroom more relaxing for those who need that. My daughter sleeps with a whirring fan full in her face, even in winter! For the rest of us, silence is golden. A good pair of earplugs can be just what we need.

GET UP: If you are struggling to fall asleep, don't lie in bed for hours on end. Instead, get up, do something else for twenty minutes, then try to sleep again.

Walter Hooper was C.S. Lewis' personal secretary. He found a place of rest in the middle of the noise and training for battle. He used to read small snatches of the book *Miracles* on the firing range at army training in Fort Jackson. Like him, we can also find rest in the busyness. Colossians 3:15 (NIV) says, "Let the peace of Christ rule in your hearts, since as members of one body you were called to peace. And be thankful."

We have a calling to peace and peacefulness. Resting is a way of exercising our faith in the control of God. In practical terms, extreme activity, sleeplessness and anxious thoughts shows a very human lack of faith. Fear leaves God's power out of the picture and forgets that God is almighty even (and especially) in our weaknesses. It is helpful to remember that if you are in God's will and your work is His assignment for you, it will have a heavenly rest schedule attached! This is awesome news!

Contentment

We are a generation that needs to look at our contentment levels carefully.

So many of the school pupils, and older people, I talk with are generally dissatisfied with what life offers them. They want more of everything. Australian Comedian Barry Humphreys, who plays the famous figure Dame Edna Everage, began his autobiography with these rather forlorn words,

"I have always wanted more. I never had enough milk or money or socks or sex or holidays or first editions or gramophone records or free meals or real friends or guiltless pleasure or neckties or applause or unquestioning love or persimmons. Of course, I have always had more than my share of these commodities, but it always left me with a vague feeling of unfulfilment: where was the rest?"

Our fast-paced society discourages any kind of contentment. Our eyes are bombarded with adverts encouraging high spending on new products, toys, services and gadgets. We are assured that we need more expensive face cream, a faster car and better internet access in order to be fulfilled, happy and successful. And we all buy into the lie. Proverbs 23:4-5 (NIV) warns us:

"Do not wear yourself out to get rich;
do not trust your own cleverness.
Cast but a glance at riches, and they are gone,
for they will surely sprout wings
and fly off to the sky like an eagle."

It is possible to be content with what we have.

In my work, I sometimes encourage anxious pupils to list the contents of their lives – to write an inventory, if you like – of all they have. It is incredible that 100% of them start with their possessions, never their health or their ability to sit, stand, think, move or run. I have to remind them about those things! The truth is that we take much of what we have, or can do, for granted. It is only when those things are pointed out, threatened or removed, that we truly notice them and long for them.

It is true that none of us remember to thank God that we can swallow, until we get tonsillitis!

A huge personal event such as a bereavement or a change in

employment status can have life-changing implications for us. Goals that we have thought previously to be important, pale into insignificance as other REAL challenges rise to the surface. I talk about this a lot in my book on loss, *Good Grief*.

In whatever season of life we find ourselves, it can be helpful to write a "Content Page" of our lives. It shows us what we have to be thankful for and helps us to be more aware of all God has blessed us with. When we are *content* with what we have, we won't be begging for more. A contented heart is a heart at rest. It is so healthy to take time out to look for the hidden ways God's goodness is at work in our lives and be intentional about thanking Him for those personal blessings.

Why not create your own *contents page* today?

Planning to rest

If you are anything like me, planning to rest can feel like hard work! In order to get any rest, I need to fight it into my diary and allow it to remain there, uncontested. Then I need to actually take the rest when it is scheduled and not bypass it, feeling that I'm too busy for it. All kinds of rest will involve advance planning. Part of the invitation of rest requires me to work first. If I am to have any hope of enjoying a Sabbath rest, I will need to set aside time at other points in the week to get all my routine jobs done.

Just today I discovered the long list of things the children needed to eat, do and wear that I had written for my parents-in-law when Jon and I once went away for a weekend. It took time to write it and cook meals to leave in the freezer for them all. It felt like hard work! But it was totally worth it.

Don't forget. Rest is fun! Taking time out to be with God and others is pleasurable for us. It says in Psalm 16:11 (ESV),

"You make known to me the path of life; in your presence there is fullness of joy; at your right hand are pleasures forevermore."

I often meet people who are 100% restless. Even when they are sitting "still" they are tapping, twitching or moving in some way. They don't have fullness of joy. They have the emptiness of human misery. Their true selves are masked by a warring crowd of busy noise. It is as if, as Portuguese poet Fernando Pessoa writes, their "soul is impatient with itself, as with a bothersome child; its restlessness keeps growing and is forever the same."

Our true identity is in Christ. Until we discover this, there won't be that wonderful feeling of "coming home rest" that each of us so desperately need. St Augustine of Hippo summed this up beautifully when he wrote this truth around AD 386:

"Thou hast made us for thyself, O Lord, and our heart is restless until it finds its rest in thee."

Rest Reflections:

- Am I quick to take offence at the moment? Are my patience levels low? Why is this? How can I address it?
- Do I struggle to sleep? If so, in what practical ways could I change my routines?
- Where in my body can I see physical signs of lack of rest? What can I do about that?
- Can I see areas of my life where I am lacking joy or gratefulness? Can I make a "contents page" today?
- Read Haggai 1:5-9 (NIV) below. What personal challenges do these verses contain for me? What will I do about them?

"Now this is what the Lord Almighty says: 'Give careful thought to your ways. You have planted much, but harvested little. You eat, but never have enough. You drink, but never have your fill. You put on clothes, but are not warm. You earn wages, only to put them in a purse with holes in it.'

This is what the Lord Almighty says: 'Give careful thought to your ways. Go up into the mountains and bring down timber and build my house, so that I may take pleasure in it and be honored,' says the Lord. 'You expected much, but see, it turned out to be little. What you brought home, I blew away. Why?' declares the Lord Almighty. 'Because of my house, which remains a ruin, while each of you is busy with your own house.'"

Chapter Six

Perspective: Mary & Martha

"Rest provides fine-tuning for hearing God's messages amidst
the static of life."
– Shelly Miller

I'm not proud of this, but I can sometimes have a rather ugly tendency towards motherly martyrdom. In my head, or even sometimes out loud, I can find myself saying phrases like, "What did your last slave die of? Exhaustion? I don't make all the mess round here, but I certainly get to clean it up!" I can feel like everybody else is just having a good time while I am left to do all the work. Then I vent my outbursts further by hoovering in very short, angry sweeps of the carpet. Or I wipe surfaces unnecessarily quickly whilst my poor family are at a loss as to what to say.

Maybe you are much more patient and controlled than me and never do anything similar?! Or maybe you just have a cleaner!

The following monologue, based on the story of Mary and Martha found in Luke 10:38, is one that has a great deal of that kind of Martyr/Martha attitude in it. I hope you find it a useful retelling and re-imagining of a set of verses that may be really very familiar to you. The following is based on Luke 10:38-42

The Empty Cushion

I woke up early that day. We'd heard the night before that Jesus might be coming to Bethany. So, I was up before dawn, frantically sweeping and tidying the house. Everything had to be perfect for Jesus. Jesus was, no... *is*, our friend. He's amazing. He's just so unique. He is the Master. Our Teacher. The Lord. So, of course, I wanted things to be right.

My darling sister Mary, on the other hand, she was... dawdling. It took her ages to eat her breakfast and she sang little lines from half a song as she day dreamed. She stroked the dog from next door and even tried to make me dance with her broom.

"No! No! No!" I had said. "Positively no dancing. He could be here any time this afternoon. Jesus. *Here*. We need to be ready Mary!"

"What does it matter?" Mary had answered. "He's not here to see how well scrubbed the table is. Or how nicely we've tidied up. He just wants to sit and chat to us."

I sighed deeply. I wanted to give Mary a piece of my mind. But I held it in. She is my younger sister. 10 years my junior. She doesn't really know how hard it is to keep a house. I had to be her mother after our own mother died. Mary has no clue what it is like to be a proper grown up. How difficult it is to keep it all together.

She aggravated me that day, just by being under my feet, and being so... well, cheerful. So, I sent her to the market, early, before the sun got too hot. I needed more flour for the bread and a few other things. Most of all, I needed space. I carefully wrote her a list.

Ten minutes after she'd gone, when I'd finished making the beds and putting away the clothes, I noticed that the list was still lying on the table. Typical Mary!

"She's hopeless!" I'd said out loud. But smiling a little, all the same.

When she got back, finally, after what seemed like far too long, she pushed open the door with a shout. "Jesus is coming up the hill! He's here!" Without even facing me, Mary threw the bag of flour and a few coppers on to the table. She was full of joy and immediately ran to meet him. But I went into a mild panic. The beads of sweat that had formed across my brow as I was cleaning now fell. I wasn't fit to be seen. I felt filthy, resentful, hot and cross. The food was only just in the pot and wasn't going to be ready on time. This was not what I had imagined. I saw the dress laid out on my bed, the one I was going to wear when he arrived. I saw the clean headscarf. All waiting, neatly folded... pointlessly. I had no time to put them on now.

I went to greet him, a little slower than usual. I knelt down to put water out for his feet, but instead he lifted my face from the floor. He threw his arms around me and hugged me.

"Martha!" he said. "Dear Martha." But I pulled away – far too early. I was ashamed of how sweaty and dirty I felt. I hadn't even washed.

Jesus rinsed his tired feet in the bowl.

"It's so good to see you both," he said. "How are you?"

Mary led Jesus to sit down. She began to talk to him about things that didn't matter. She chattered away as he drank some water, smiling and occasionally looking over at me.

"Can I get you some more?" I asked, noticing he'd put his cup down. I glared at Mary who annoyed me even more by not even noticing I was glaring at *her*.

"I'm fine," said Jesus. "Thank you, Martha."

"I will have a drink please my love," said Mary, absent-mindedly, not taking her eyes off Jesus.

"Oh, you'll have a drink will you?" I fumed inwardly. I went back over to the small kitchen area of our one-room home. I grabbed a cup and filled it roughly with water. It spilt out over my hand. I handed it to her jerkily, with gritted teeth. I actually wanted to throw it over her silly head. But I kept my temper. Just.

The smell from the meal cooking in the pot made me realise I'd been too busy to eat any breakfast. My tummy growled. I pressed my apron hard against it and started to turn out the bread and knead the mixture angrily. Every pummel found energy in my blackened mood.

"Why. Do. I. Have. To. Do. It. All?" I mouthed inwardly.

"Why does she *never* help me?"

I heard them laugh together. I felt left out. I couldn't hear exactly what he was saying. They were having fun and I was on my own. I checked the pot again and slammed down the lid. A little too hard. It made a loud noise.

Jesus turned to me, his piercing eyes seeing everything. Seeing through me. I tried to look away in case a dangerous tear escaped.

"Are you OK, Martha? Come and sit down," he whispered.

"I'm just making dinner," I said. Muttering under my breath, "Someone has to. It won't be long."

Mary sat on a cushion at Jesus' feet. He kept looking over to me as he spoke, trying to include me. I made as much noise as I could. I don't even know why. I was desperate to hear him. See him. Know him. And feel known by him. But I was too wound up, too angry, too hurt. My sister was doing nothing to help me. As usual.

"Don't you care that I am doing all the work?" I said finally, spitting the words out with venom.

Jesus stopped and looked at me. Mary was shocked. Sad. Embarrassed. I was red faced. Red with anger, red with shame, red with jealousy and red with heat.

"Tell my sister to come and help me!" I sobbed, tears stinging the back of my eyes. "Doesn't it seem unfair to you that she just sits there listening to you while I do all the work?" The voice of loud blame rose from my chest.

But Jesus came to me. He held out his hands to mine.

"Martha, my dear, dear friend. You are so upset over these small details. You care about the lamb stew and the bread. You care that the house looks perfect and that you look nice to welcome me. And I love that. But there is really only one thing to be concerned about here. Just one thing. Mary has discovered it and it won't be taken away from her."

I choked back my tears. Defeated by his smile, I went and sat down. Something eternal was in the making. But it wasn't in the kitchen. The stew bubbled happily, unwatched and unchecked. The bread baked just as well without me looking at it every few seconds. I breathed deeply. I took the empty cushion and joined my sister where I belonged. You see it matters, not just that we sit, but that we sit *there* – at his feet."

I found that piece challenging to think through and write because it exposed a great deal of both my innate personality and my problem. I know that I need to be more like Mary, but I find myself thinking, acting and behaving much more readily like her sister. It made me ask the question: "Are there things I am doing that God never intended me to do?"

What about you?

Martha often gets a bad press.

But not from me.

I understand her and have great sympathy with her point of view. I am often an activist. I see a need and want to do something about it. I can get frustrated when people just sit about and look holy. But Martha is the sleeves-rolled-up girl, grasping her salad servers. I can see her clearly. The George Forman grill is on high, the dishwasher is beeping, the washing machine is whirring. The kettle is on. The book about modern slavery is half finished on the side. The emails are flying in. The talk is nearly written. Whatsapp messages are pouring onto her phone. She has it all going on.

I know what life like *that* is like. I can be like Martha. Maybe you can too.

But I also understand Mary. She's been listening to a podcast on the "Ten most beautiful blessings of restfulness". She has just downloaded the new Bethel CD from iTunes. She is booked into a conference on the new spiritual discipline of peaceful contemplative prayer with pilates at a silent retreat centre in Cornwall, with watercolour painting in the evenings. She hugs strangers on trains. She laughs and cries at adverts. She is joyful. She is little.

I also know what life like *that* is like. I can be like Mary. Maybe you can too. I am a worshipper at heart. I can spend hours praying and singing and forget my other responsibilities. There is a bit of both of them in me.

I think that there is a bit of both of them in you too. And the reason is because they represent two facets of our divinely-made human nature. We were made for restful worship. We were also made to work.

I am aware that what I am sharing with you is very simple, but I hope it's profound too.

God is in our worship, the Mary part of us, but He's also in our work, the Martha part. In fact, the Hebrew word *Avodah* (which sounds like a Star Wars character, I know!) is actually the translation of the Hebrew word for "worship" and "work". It means both. Worshipful work.

Let me encourage you to knead those two words together today like bread. Worship and work. Work and worship. Avodah.

I recently watched a film online. Part of the script said,

"We live in a Martha world; we're troubled, we're anxious, and we're distracted. But God built this world to be a Mary world with Martha moments. When sin entered the world, it turned into a Martha world in which we have to fight for Mary moments."

I really agree with that. Do you? I think it often feels like a fight to be centred and at peace. I know that my day is clunky when my work and my worship feel separate and stressful. When praying becomes a chore, my work does too. I think being at rest means that our work and our worship naturally intertwine, like friends. More than this, like sisters. They rely on one another.

On days when both become our offering and both become holy, those are great days. Those are high-five, peace-filled Mary and Martha days. Where both offerings become acceptable to God and to us. But one has to come from the other.

Our best work, my best work and yours, has to come from a place of space and worship. Of deep breath and openness.

Writer Joanna Weaver wrote in her book *Having a Mary Heart in a Martha World*,

"Jesus' words to Martha are the words He wants to speak to your heart and mine: 'You are worried and upset about many things, but only one thing is needed.' The 'one thing' is not found in doing more. It's found by sitting at His feet.'"

As a writer, there are days when I feel a real inspiration block. I write a few words, but they seem turgid and lacking in form. I tap away more at the delete button than anything else. I find this especially the case if I am busy and have deadlines to meet. But if I pray and spend time with God, I find I am grateful and thankful. My heart is a more spacious place and I find His words flowing through me with ease.

The temptation is to cut down on the prayers when I'm busy. But I am learning that these are the times I need them the most. ALSO, and this is a weird but true thing, in prayer, time stretches out. I will then seem to have more time, not less. I become more productive. This is part of what it means for me when Jesus said, "Seek first the kingdom and everything else will be added to you…" (Matthew 6:33).

Countless times when I have done that – sought His face first – He has added to me. Even stretched out the hours for me. I have noticed that my mind is more effective when it has worshipped. Why? Because this is what my mind was made to do. To commune with God. Make peace with Him. Go placidly.

Work won't make as much sense to me if it is taken out of the context of worship.

Jesus accepted and understood both Martha and Mary. He loved both the sisters. But He wanted what Mary was bringing Him and recognised that her attitude to her day was the blessed one. It was her priority that He encouraged.

Food is important, but our faith is more so. That nourishes us more than our bread. The rhythm of our day is supposed to be Mary first, then Martha. Spend time with Jesus, then with others. Pray first, then work. Read the Bible, then do the washing up. Sing before the food shop (or at least on the way). When we worship like Mary, we will work more effectively.

Years ago, I benefitted massively from spending time with some monks at Aylesford Priory who taught me how to pray contemplatively whilst they worked. I watched them pray for the person whose habit they were ironing. I saw them as they were pulling up weeds in the garden, asking God to show them the rubbish in their own hearts. Everything became an opportunity to pray. I'm not saying I remember to do that all the time. I really don't! But I do find it helpful to call to mind that I can. I can hoover and ask God to clear out anything from my house that does not belong to Him. I can cook a meal and pray it nourishes our bodies. I can make a bed and pray for the dreams of my children.

This time taught me how to pray more effectively through my day. It taught me to want Mary's heart but Martha's hands. The fact is, sometimes we serve others best simply by being present with them.

Recently, I have been interested by the use of the Danish word *Hygge* (pronounced hue-guh) coming into common parlance. The word means something of a special, cosy or charming moment. It is not about adopting a certain lifestyle or buying anything in particular. It has nothing to do with interior design or special food. Being *hygge* requires a conscious appreciation, a deliberate slowness. It is about not just being present in the moment, but enjoying that time in your life and sharing it with others. I think *hygge* describes Mary's attitude remarkably well.

Preventing burnout

Because we are finite and weak, we can all too soon empty ourselves when we serve and give sacrificially. Like Martha, I am sure all of us know someone who has pushed themselves to this level of fatigue. Perhaps it is something you yourself are all too familiar with?

Psychology researcher Herbert Freudenburger was the first person to coin the term "burnout". In his study of workers, he found that the symptoms of exhaustion due to excessive work demands led to some physical problems, like sleeplessness and headaches. He also observed that burnt-out people were "quick to anger" (as we talked about in the last chapter) and suffered from "closed thinking". He observed that a person with burnout "looks, acts, and seems depressed."

I have noticed that when people within a Christian community reach exhaustion and burnout, something significant is lost. When a pastor or leader loses sight of healthy work/life boundaries, often that person will need extreme rest and total relaxation in order to fully recover. Their emotional weariness harms the successful functioning of those around them. Others take the strain of their workload as they fight to regain control. The truth is, burnout and breakdown have far-reaching implications for everyone who loves or relies on that person.

It is important to remember that the Body of Christ is harmed when people do not rest fully.

So how can we prevent martyr exhaustion and Martha-like fatigue happening to us? E.F. Schumacker said,

> "Any intelligent fool can make things bigger, more complex, and more violent. It takes a touch of genius – and a lot of courage – to move in the opposite direction."

A biblical perspective is that resting and closeness with God fills us, so that we can serve with strength and joy. Rest like this protects, maintains and lengthens whatever God has called us to do for Him. Rest stops us from over reaching and breaking down. It ensures we do things well, with a good attitude that is free from resentment. I think rest like this looks similar to what we read in Psalm 71:5-8 (NIV) which says,

> "For you have been my hope, Sovereign Lord,
> my confidence since my youth.
> From birth I have relied on you;
> you brought me forth from my mother's womb.
> I will ever praise you. I have become a sign to many;
> you are my strong refuge.
> My mouth is filled with your praise,
> declaring your splendour all day long."

Recently, I had the chance to have a significant conversation with a pastor who had suffered from burnout. I asked him:

How did you know you were on the edge of a break down?
"I found myself not caring about things that had really mattered to me before. I was easily angered and irritated."

What happened?

"I had to stop. I needed total rest from my ministry. Fortunately, I had an amazing team around me, so I knew that I could have time out without things falling down around me."

What steps did you take?

"I got myself a counsellor who helped me talk through how I was feeling. I realised that I had lost my 'first love'. I had simply been going through the motions for a long time. I had left my passion behind because I was overseeing things rather than actually doing them."

What were your thoughts at this time?

"My self-talk was awful! The things I was allowing myself to say about me were hugely destructive. I had to make some changes in that area. I had to ask myself, 'What would God say over me today?'"

What practical steps did you take as a result?

"I started writing a journal. It was really helpful for me to make a note of all I was thinking and the questions I was asking. I still go back to that journal now. It is very precious to me.

I also began taking exercise and looking after my body. I think I had neglected myself for a long time. For me, walking was a life-saver.

I surrounded myself with good people and close friends who prayed with me and helped me to recover."

Maybe you can relate to this short testimony? I'm glad to say that the guy in question is back in business! But he's not back in *busyness*. He has learnt the hard lesson that for too long he had been working *for* Jesus, but not working and partnering *with* Him. Our tiredness matters deeply to God. He knows how we are doing and what we need.

Selah

The Bible uses the unusual word "Selah" seventy-four times. The actual meaning of the word is not fully known, but there are various interpretations offered to us. Some scholars think that the word is a musical mark of some kind, given to the person in charge of sung worship. The Amplified version of the Bible interestingly translates the word as "pause and think of that". Thirty-one of the thirty-nine Psalms with the caption "To the choir master" also make use of the word Selah. This may mean that the word indicates a break in the song, like a "rest" in music notation. But some Jewish leaders think it to be a stronger inference than just to *stop*. They think it more likely means "Stop and listen" (exactly what we see Mary doing in the story we have just focused on). A further interpretation claims that Selah originates from the Hebrew root word *Salah* meaning "to hang" and "to measure" or "weigh". Whatever its original meaning, it is interesting to find it so often in worship-centred Scripture.

We all need to weigh up how we live. We need to allow time to stop, listen and to offer pause and reflection. Selah rest gives us that very chance. It presents us with the courage to discover deeper truth and weigh the very words of God.

What are the side-effects of rest?

1. Rest brings better perspective. It enables us to see things clearly, as they really are. Jesus didn't want Martha to "lose sight" of that which was better.

2. Rest brings greater priority. Jesus encouraged Martha to do one thing, not dabble in 40 things. Joyce Meyer said, "Learning what to do and when to do it is a very key issue, because when we do the right thing at the wrong time, it becomes the wrong thing to do."

3. Rest brings revelation and promise. In rest we are given the power, presence and purposes of God. Jeremiah 33:3 (ESV) says, "Call to me and I will answer you, and will tell you great and hidden things that you have not known."

4. Rest brings peace. Knowing that we have done what we were asked to do brings a sense of deep satisfaction and calm.

5. Rest is found in the person of Jesus Himself. Jesus calls us to Himself – not just to read a great book or spend more time in the gym. Rest is not an event, it is a *person*. Jesus speaks to us and says, "Come to me, come with me. I will give you rest." He invites us to enter His rest by coming into proximity with HIM. John 7:37 says that,

> "On the last and greatest day of the feast, Jesus stood up and called out in a loud voice, 'If anyone is thirsty, let him come to Me and drink.'"

In short, rest fuels what God has called us to do, and ensures we do it well.

"It is the vigorous use of idle time that will broaden your education, make you a more efficient specialist, a happier man, a more useful citizen. It will help you understand the rest of the world and make you more resourceful." – Wilder Penfield

Rest Reflections:

- In what ways do I identify with the Mary and Martha story?
- What priorities am I holding at the moment? Are they the right ones?
- Am I in danger of burnout? Do I suffer from "closed" or negative thinking? What could I do about this?
- Have I lost my first love? What changes could I make to recover?
- Do I struggle to say no to things I am asked to do, even if they compromise my time/energy/ efficiency?
- If Jesus were to look at my life right now, would He see it characterised by "one thing" or many half-done things?

Chapter Seven

Still Waters

A closer look at Psalm 23

"The word 'silent' contains the same letters
as the word 'listen'."

Switched off

For a short while, when I was 9, I played 3rd Trumpet in my school orchestra. It was often the most mind-sappingly dull part EVER – just the occasional bass note to go alongside the melody. I didn't last long. I was not very good at counting the rests and, invariably, I would come in at the wrong time, much to the consternation of my music teacher.

When my husband, Jon, was in the sixth-form, he was in a play. One night, he asked a friend (offstage) which scene they were up to and found out, to his horror, that it was one in which he should have been on stage! He had to casually wander through the wings and make it look like he meant it! But then he had no idea where they were up to, or whether he was meant to speak. I believe his fellow actors were less than delighted.

I remember one day when my kettle didn't switch itself off.

There was a tea towel trapped underneath the switch. It couldn't shut off, even if it had wanted to. It boiled dry and blew all the kitchen fuses. It just kept boiling the water constantly until it had all gone.

There is something dangerous about being *on* when we should be *off* and *off* when we should be *on*.

We need to know which is which.

Leaving yourself ON constantly will have the same effect. You will "boil dry" and likely deeply affect the lives of those around you. So, let me ask you a question: Is your behaviour forcing you, your kids, your family or your employees to stay "switched on" for too long? Have you trapped them into not being allowed to turn off?

One of the most famous psalms in the Bible has much to teach us about switching off. I didn't know, until recently, that this psalm was sung in the early Church when people were getting baptised. This is noteworthy. Why? Because it signifies a fresh start and a new perspective. I pray it give us both as we look at it together.

Take some time now to re-read this beautiful passage with me. It may help to say it out loud.

"The Lord is my shepherd; I shall not want.
He makes me lie down in green pastures.
He leads me beside still waters.
He restores my soul.
He leads me in paths of righteousness
for his name's sake.
Even though I walk through the valley of the shadow of death,
I will fear no evil,
for you are with me;

your rod and your staff,
they comfort me.
You prepare a table before me
in the presence of my enemies;
you anoint my head with oil;
my cup overflows.
Surely goodness and mercy shall follow me
all the days of my life,
and I shall dwell in the house of the Lord
forever." (Psalm 23 ESV)

The ultimate relationship

As a young child, I would love to climb into my Grandma's huge bed in the morning and let her tell me a story. I would lie there with my eyes tightly shut, imagining it all in my head. One of the most vivid stories that had the biggest impact on my faith as a child was a sombre one about a young boy. I don't know where Grandma first heard this tale, or even whether it was true. But for me, it gave a unique insight into the relationship it was possible to have with Jesus.

The story (in a much more condensed form than my Grandma would tell me!) went like this:

After the death of his parents, a little boy went to stay with his aged grandfather who lived in the Scottish highlands and worked as a shepherd. His grandfather was a strong Christian man who told him many of the stories in the Bible, especially tales of the great shepherds – Moses, David and Abraham. The little boy loved to hear about the best of all the shepherds, Jesus. Although he couldn't read, the grandfather taught him a simple way to remember five lovely words about the Good Shepherd from Psalm 23 verse 1. The little boy would say, "The Lord is my shepherd," pointing to a separate finger as he said each word. When he got to the fourth finger he would hold it tightly, saying the word "my" with a smile.

As the boy grew older, he was able to take the sheep by himself to the highlands to find fresh grass, while his grandfather napped by the fire. One afternoon the weather changed dramatically and the grandfather became anxious. He went out to search for the boy, but was soon forced to return to his cottage because of the deep snow.

The following day the man went out again to see if he could find his grandson. He searched and searched, becoming more fearful with every step. Then, all of a sudden, he came across a strange mound in the snow. There, buried under fresh snowfall was his grandson, frozen to death. The grandfather fell to his knees and wept his heart out. But then he noticed something odd about the way the boy was lying. He saw that the lad's hands were clasped. As he brushed the snow away from the freezing fingers, he could clearly see that the boy had died, gripping the fourth finger of his left hand.

As you might imagine, tears would roll down my cheeks as I heard this familiar story. And for me, ever since, Psalm 23 has always been MY psalm about MY Saviour.

"The Lord is my shepherd; I shall not want"
The story is told of a famous orator and actor who was known for his dramatic recital of Psalm 23. The crowd would burst into thunderous applause as he spoke the words, using his powerfully-trained, booming voice. One evening, just before he was due to give his usual recital, a young man asked if he could

say the words instead. The actor was surprised, but invited the youth to come up to the stage. Quietly, the man began to speak the words of the psalm. When he had finished, there was no clapping. No one rose to their feet. There was only the gentle sound of soft weeping from the audience.

Amazed by what he had just witnessed, the actor spoke to the man, incredulously. "How did you do that? I have been reciting that psalm for years and have never seen an audience cry as they did tonight. What is your secret?"

The young man humbly turned to the actor.

"Well sir, you know the psalm, but I know the Shepherd."

Throughout the Bible, God speaks of Himself, and other leaders he appoints, as shepherds. A *good* shepherd is one that provides all that the sheep need in terms of nourishment, refreshment and protection. But a *godly* shepherd is also far more than this. In Psalm 78:72 we see how David is described as having both character and competence.

"And David shepherded them with integrity of heart; with skillful hands he led them."

Integrity of heart and skillful hands are both important. They are a picture of Jesus. In John 10 Jesus speaks of Himself as being the ultimate Good Shepherd. John 10:7-10 (AMP) tells us,

"So, Jesus said again, 'I assure you and most solemnly say to you, I am the Door for the sheep [leading to life]. All who came before Me [as false messiahs and self-appointed leaders] are thieves and robbers, but the [true] sheep did not hear them. I am the Door; anyone who enters through Me will be saved [and will live forever], and will go in and out [freely], and find pasture (spiritual security). The thief comes only in order to steal and kill and destroy. I came that they may have and enjoy life, and have it in abundance [to the full, till it overflows]."

With Jesus as our guide, we have everything we could ever need, in abundance. He shows us how to live. Not by giving us instructions and leaving us to it, but by going ahead of us, as a wise, kind, sacrificial leader.

We know that in reality Jesus was homeless. Matthew 8:19-20 says,

"Then a certain scribe came and said to Him, 'Teacher, I will follow You wherever You go.' And Jesus said to him, 'Foxes have holes and birds of the air have nests, but the Son of Man has nowhere to lay His head.'" (NKJV)

Jesus chooses, as our Shepherd, to make His home with us and, crucially, *in us*.

He makes me lie down

Elephants only need 4 hours. Sloths need 16. Extraordinarily, dolphins have unihemispheric heads, which means one side of their brains can be asleep whilst the other side is awake! But every creature on earth needs some kind of rest period.

We can't live without it, yet millions of us struggle to get enough shut-eye.

Sleep expert Dr Sophie Bostock said,

"Just in the last five years we've had research revealing the impact of sleep on risk of cognitive decline, for example, dementia, high blood pressure and the common cold. You're actually four times more likely to get a cold if you get fewer than seven hours sleep."

As a society, we are often exhausted and sleep-deprived. I have been amazed and amused to find that there are many rather bizarre suggestions available online which supposedly promote better sleep. For example, did you know that popping a bit of grass-fed butter into your herbal tea before bed is meant to help you sleep? (in my case, that remedy is far more likely to bring on indigestion, or acne!) There is also a perfectly genuine school of thought that tells you to sleep on special "earthing" sheets that are connected to the ground outside via an expensive pipe. These sheets promise to connect us with the earth's natural energy which apparently has untold health benefits.

There are also sites dedicated to the practice of eating activated charcoal to detox the body; going barefoot outdoors; and even getting red lights fitted that are the least damaging for the circadian rhythm (although they might cause some questions for the neighbours!) There are many eccentric things we will try in order to help us rest.

Why are we so tired?

I've written in a previous chapter about the disappearing boundaries between our work and home lives. Quite often, our labours will bleed into our leisure with no obvious distinction between the two. Our laptop and phone screens are the universal portal for our work, learning, social life, shopping, gaming, viewing and communication. When we tap away on a screen we could be ordering a take away, buying a book, betting on a gambling site or Skyping our nephew.

In the old days when there were just four channels on the TV, and even into the 1980s, all television broadcasting stopped just after midnight. On the BBC, a plummy voice would wish you, "A good night" and remind you to turn off your TV set. Then a clock would be shown and the National Anthem would play.

This prompted you to go to bed. But now, with the huge wash of programming "on demand", there is no such communal nudge.

I regularly meet pupils who have gorged themselves on junk food, junk watching and junk social media, whose red eyes stare at me vacuously as they struggle to remember what day it is.

The art of napping

It has fallen out of favour and is considered to be something for the elderly or for children in nursery settings, but I am a big fan of "napping". Naps, or short sleeps, are proven to increase our alertness and have many benefits. Lots of different kinds of research shows that napping improves the elasticity of our memory and enhances cognitive function. As I have been researching, I have found that many different, highly productive people in history and today find a nap a powerful tool for their personal restoration.

Perhaps one of the most famous nappers in history was Winston Churchill. This Prime Minister regarded his daily naps as totally essential to the war effort. His valet, Frank Sawyers, said, "It is one of the inflexible rules of Mr Churchill's daily routine that he should not miss this rest." Naps were so important to him that he even kept a bed in the Houses of Parliament.

Churchill would begin the day around 7am, sitting up in bed, with a specially adapted lap tray, which was like a mini writing desk. On this, his staff would place all the correspondence, memos and letters that he would need to read and sign that morning. He would then get up, get dressed into one of his famous chalk-striped suits, and have a light breakfast. Only then would he make an appearance at the War Cabinet room, or attend meetings, or involve himself in public appearances.

At about five o'clock each day Churchill would take a solid one-hour nap, in freshly ironed pyjamas or the unusual romper suit-zipped onesies he designed. Then he would work again until he went to bed at midnight, leaving his staff very strict instructions that he should not be disturbed for any reason, other than that the British Isles was actually being invaded!

Churchill was not a young man when he took office. He understood that, at the age of 66, frequent and planned rest was vital to his function. He knew from his military background that damaged sleep led to poor situational awareness and impaired decision making.

Concerning his naps, Churchill is reported to have said, "You must sleep some time between lunch and dinner, and no half-way measures. Take off your clothes and get into bed. That's what I always do. Don't think you will be doing less work because you sleep during the day. That's a foolish notion held by people who have no imagination. You will be able to accomplish more. You get two days in one – well, at least one and a half, I'm sure. When the war started, I had to sleep during the day because that was the only way I could cope with my responsibilities."

It is true to say that Adolf Hitler, a much younger man than Churchill, in contrast, tried to stay up for days at a time, on a cocktail of drugs.

A short nap of even 20-30 minutes can help to improve our mood, alertness and performance. Thomas Edison's personal secretary, Alfred Tate, called his naps Edison's secret weapon and declared that, "his genius for sleep availed his genius for invention."

Many creative people also claim that sleep – in particular their dreams – have helped them in their careers. For example, Paul Mcartney wrote the song Yesterday in his sleep. Golfer, Jack Nicklaus also described a dream that helped him with his golf swing. Lead singer of Fleetwood Mac, Christine McVie penned *Songbird* in just half an hour when she woke up in the night with it fully-formed in her head. She said, "I had a little transistorized electric piano next to my bed and I woke up one night at about 3.30am and started playing it. I had all the words, melody chords in about 30 minutes. It was like a gift from the angels."

Perhaps you could take a leaf out of their book and try taking a nap next time you feel shattered?

In green pastures

As a child, I remember farmers "fallowing" fields: letting cattle or sheep graze the land and fertilise it naturally. Fallow fields were traditionally used by farmers to maintain the natural productivity of their land. Leaving a field fallow rebalanced the soil's nutrients and broke pest and crop disease cycles. It enabled worms to produce castings which enriched the soil with microbes and fungi. This gave life, energy and the potential of growth to the soil.

Until 1939 we had 800,000 hectares of rotational fallowing in the UK. But this began to be seen as "uneconomic" and even wasteful. More recent EU agricultural policies meant farmers could no longer leave as much set-aside or fallow land. Land owners resorted to using strong, unnatural pesticides and herbicides on the tired ground in an attempt to maximise its yield. The result was that the soil deteriorated and began to need even more artificial fertiliser.

I believe this is a picture of what can happen to us.

God's desire for us is that we are led into green pastures, into areas that are productive, fruitful, beautiful and restful for us. But so often we fight against Him. We try and consume food, atmospheres, relationships and life choices that are not healthy for us. We don't rest well and then need help to sleep. We fill our minds with stressful, chaotic activity and then feel too tired to pray. As the margins around our lives become less, there is a reduced amount of space for fun, compassion, creativity and commitment.

There seems to be some irony in the "green pastures" phrase. When we think of the land of Israel, I don't think many of us picture lush, verdant meadows. In reality, most of the grass there consists of clumps set in desert-like, rocky terrain. This tells me something about what is in David's mind as he writes. He is telling me that God will provide for me in ways that are deeper than simply using natural resources. He will give me something supernatural and extraordinary, in ways that my earthly life cannot normally provide.

I have noticed this time and time again. When I prayed for a child, He gave me four. When I prayed for work, He gave me favour with future employers. When I prayed for creativity, He gave me dreams that came true. God supernaturally gives us MORE than we expect, deserve or imagine. His green pastures are lavish, abundant and life giving.

But, as with so much in life, our POSITIONING is so key. Where we lie is vitally important. We are not lying in a place of discomfort or lack, but somewhere connected to provision, blessing and honour. A sheep will not lie down if it is scared. Sheep are skittish, nervous creatures who are easily startled. God is inviting us here into a place where we are content to know He is guiding, providing and caring for us. There is no safer place than this!

When we had our twins, I remember that our church at the time cooked for us for an amazing six weeks! We felt so loved and blessed. One evening it was the turn of a sweet, single lady to bring us our tea. She arrived apologetically with two full Tesco bags. She told us that she wasn't very good at cooking, so had bought us ready meals. We were so exhausted that we were just grateful for anything. After she'd left we unpacked all the items. Every single one was from that supermarket's "finest" range. As people on low income and a tight budget, we never ate food like this. Our usual food was wholesome... but cheap! It sounds crazy, but I can still recall the taste of that champagne and strawberry mousse she bought me that day – and this was 12 years ago!

God knows exactly what kind of diet each of His sheep need. He is not going to give you the same thing He gives me, but the promise is that it will be the best, "Heaven's finest" range.

Isaiah 55:2 (NLT) says,

"Why spend your money on food that does not give you strength?
Why pay for food that does you no good?
Listen to me, and you will eat what is good.
You will enjoy the finest food."

He leads me beside still waters

I remember reading something recently about this verse that made me think. A student had studied this phrase and decided that she didn't want to be led to "still water". Why? Because she had grown up near a stagnant pond that was a hive of germs and problems for her local community. It was a place where Malaria and Dengue fever could thrive and where mosquitos bred. She had to be shown the true meaning of this phrase.

The still water God offers us is not putrid or inactive in any way. In fact, in contrast, it is life-giving and nourishing. In Hebrew, the words for "still waters" in Psalm 23:2b are *Mai Menochot*, literally meaning "restful waters". The Good Shepherd wants to take us to places that will feed us and quench our thirst. The kind of water that He spoke of in John 4, and again in John 7, is an everlasting water that will satisfy and sustain us, always.

We are designed to be hungry and thirsty. In a physical sense, we are created to need food and water to live. We are also created with emotional and spiritual hungers. God made us to crave His presence and the life that only He offers. He also knew that we would try and quench our thirst ourselves. The Bible says in Jeremiah 2:13 (NCV),

> "My people have done two evils: They have turned away from me, the spring of living water. And they have dug their own wells, which are broken wells that cannot hold water."

Each of us try and "dig our own wells", rather than position ourselves by still waters. Maybe you have tasted this kind of life-giving water in the past, but have walked away from it. Perhaps you find yourself in a place of striving, or you feel dry and parched. Will you let me encourage you to rediscover the source of your thirst and the only way to relieve it? John 4:13-14 (TLB) says,

> "Jesus replied that people soon became thirsty again after drinking this water. 'But the water I give them,' he said, 'becomes a perpetual spring within them, watering them forever with eternal life.'"

Revelation 7:17 (NIV) gives us more of a clue about what this means:

"For the Lamb at the centre of the throne will be their shepherd; he will lead them to springs of living water. And God will wipe away every tear from their eyes."

Do you need a fresh infilling from that perpetual spring today?

He restores my soul

I have always loved old furniture. It was a passion passed on to me by my late grandma, who collected all sorts of beautiful items over a number of years. Once upon a time I had a sideline business with a friend, renovating small items of bespoke furniture. During this time, I met a wonderful local antiques expert who was part of the British Antique Furniture Restorers' Association. This organisation is a group of crafts people engaged in the authentic and correct conservation and restoration of artefacts and furniture. Brad would show me great examples of restored items that had been completed in such a way as to retain and even sometimes strengthen the value and integrity of the piece.

True restoration requires great skill, patience and knowledge. According to his naval aide, Harry Butcher, Dwight Eisenhower was working 15-18 hours a day in 1945 and had become a man whose problems frequently kept him awake at night. He asked Butcher to find him a hideout, somewhere he could recharge and rest. Butcher found a small house called Telegraph Cottage in Kingston, which was a well-kept secret. Here, General Eisenhower played golf, read cowboy novels, went horse riding and totally detached himself from the war. This became one of the reasons for his great success.

True restoration requires separation.

As our restorer, God has vast skill and knowledge to draw on.

He also knows how to lead us away to a quiet place on our own in order to help us rest and recuperate.

When God restores us, He does a first-class job. He removes fear, shame, hopelessness and pain. He rebuilds us with hope, purity, joy and peace.

He leads me in paths of righteousness for his name's sake

I have an almost unrivalled appalling sense of direction. I can lose my way easily. A couple of years ago I went to watch my children sing in our local cathedral. I don't know the centre of Manchester very well and was a little anxious about getting lost on the way in the dark. But on the tram I met up with a tall, brightly-dressed lady I recognised from the school playground. I latched onto her and her family and she guided me through the streets in such a way that I didn't even notice where I was walking. I arrived early, totally relaxed and feeling safe and at peace.

Perhaps one of the most powerful of all Bible scriptures concerning guidance is found in Proverbs 3:5-6 (AMP), which says,

> "Trust in and rely confidently on the Lord with all your heart and do not rely on your own insight or understanding. In all your ways know and acknowledge and recognise Him, and He will make your paths straight and smooth [removing obstacles that block your way]."

Do you sometimes feel as though the paths of your life are far from straight? Does it feel as though you are on a zig-zag course to nowhere? That may be due to a lack of proximity to the One who knows the path. When we come to know Jesus as our Shepherd, He reveals Himself to us in a number of different guises. One is as THE WAY. Indeed, one of the most profoundly wonderful truths Jesus said about Himself is, "I am the way" (John 14:6). We need to notice that Jesus didn't say, "I *know* the way." Or, "I will *show you* the way." No. He said I AM it.

There is great joy to be found in the presence of a companion who knows the road ahead. Psalm 32:8 tells us that God will instruct us and teach us the way we should go. But more than this, that He will counsel us and have His eyes on us as we travel. What does it mean to walk along "paths of righteousness"? I believe that staying on those kinds of paths means we behave in ways that please, reflect and glorify God.

What kind of path are you on right now? Does it have those characteristics?

Even though I walk through the valley of the shadow of death, I will fear no evil

We live in a world of shifting shadows. There are many things that, if we were to let them, could steal our peace and make us afraid. I found an anonymous version of the Antithesis of Psalm 23 which sums up some of our fears.

The clock is my dictator, I shall not rest
It makes me lie down only when exhausted
It leads me into deep depression
It hounds my soul
It leads me in circles of frenzy, for activity's sake
Even though I run frantically from task to task,
I will never get it all done,
For my ideal is with me

Deadlines and my need for approval, they drive me
They demand performance from me,
Beyond the limits of my schedule
They anoint my head with migraines
My in-basket overflows
Surely fatigue and time pressures shall follow me
All the days of my life.
And I will dwell in the bonds of frustration forever.

I don't know how that makes you feel. For many of us, fear is an ever-present part of our lives. We are afraid of what people think, afraid we are putting on weight or aging. We are afraid of our finances failing, or our health deteriorating. We are afraid of the state of our world or the future for our children. Life can be characterised by fear, pressure and stress. Fear stops us resting more than anything else. But none of this is necessary.

What a mercy this version of Psalm 23 is not true for those of us who belong to the Shepherd!

Writer Elizabeth George said,

"With the help of the Lord, you can handle life's challenges and heartaches, even the valley of the shadow of death. What comfort your fainting heart has, knowing that in those stumbling times of discouragement and despair, of depletion and seeming defeat, the Shepherd will find you... restore and 'fix' you... and follow you... until you are well on your way."

For you are with me; your rod and your staff, they comfort me
David goes out of his way in this psalm to convey the idea that our Good Shepherd provides us with protection and safety. Knowing that Jesus is fully-armed with weapons to ward off danger is

something I can sometimes forget. The rod mentioned here, which was more of a thick club, was used to scare off overland or above attack from both robbers and wild animals. The staff, or shepherd's stick, was used to protect the sheep from land-lying predators such as scorpions and snakes. The sense of both of them together creates a visual image of covering all bases. Up high and down low, we are protected.

Oswald Chambers summed this up well when he wrote,

"In the midst of the awesomeness, a touch comes, and you know it is the right hand of Jesus Christ. You know it is not the hand of restraint, correction, nor chastisement, but the right hand of the Everlasting Father. Whenever His hand is laid upon you, it gives inexpressible peace and comfort, and the sense that 'underneath are the everlasting arms', (Deuteronomy 33:27) full of support, provision, comfort and strength."

You prepare a table before me, in the presence of my enemies
Preacher Charles Spurgeon said,

"The good man has his enemies. He would not be like his Lord if he had not. If we were without enemies we might fear that we were not the friends of God, for the friendship of the world is enmity to God."

It is quite an extraordinary thing that, as God's people, we can prosper even in the very midst of our foes. The friends of God are promised to experience victory in the presence of alarm and distress. This is the proof of divine favour over us – not just that God can use all things that happen to us for our good (Romans 8:28), but that He conducts our blessing in full view of those who would dearly like us to fail (Psalm 35:2). Our attacks will look different for each of us. Our enemies, like our friends, tend to be fairly unique. Enemy assignments come in the form of appliances breaking, relationships failing, work being lost, health being compromised and many other guises that seek to steal our joy and rob us of trust.

I have had a number of interesting and powerful enemies through the years. Many of them have tried to stop me progressing in some way. It is hard when people take a dislike to us, especially when they choose to voice that.

But our vindication is promised by one who never lies. Our full triumph isn't just that we win, but that we will be seen to be winners by those who would very much prefer us to lose. It is not just that we *survive*, but that we will *thrive* in spite of our troubles. It is not just that we "make it", but that we will be increased and grown through the experiences we have faced.

You anoint my head with oil; my cup overflows
One of my dear friends recently sent me a video that made me cry with laughter. Her smallest child had climbed up onto a table, found a tub of Sudocrem antiseptic cream and liberally daubed herself and the ENITRE room with it. The thick, oily white substance was everywhere. She could not escape its greasy trail and it was very difficult to remove!

In the Bible, anointing was part of various rituals connected with worship, hospitality and kingship. Sometimes a host would anoint a guest with oil as a mark of respect and honour. When people were given an anointing, it meant that they were set apart and empowered to accomplish what God had ordained them to do (see 1 Samuel 10:6 and 16:13). God's anointing also brought with it a sense of His divine protection. No one was allowed to harm God's anointed person. Psalm 105:15 and 1 Chronicles 16:22 both say, "Do not touch my anointed ones; do my prophets no harm." The Bible is clear that there is a heavenly shield around those whom God has chosen. Don't you find this of great comfort? I do.

The phrase "My cup overflows" has sometimes been translated as "My cup runs over". A cup that runs over is one that cannot hold all that is being poured into it. By definition there is some supernatural spillage. When we are full to the brim and overflowing with joy, love and peace, it is catching. It spills out and spreads to others. I long to be known as someone who POURS themselves out for other people with that which God had first given to me. In Philippians 2:17 we see that this was Paul's ambition too:

> "But even if I am being poured out like a drink offering on the sacrifice and service coming from your faith, I am glad and rejoice with all of you."

God has set us apart for wonderful things. He has anointed us specifically and given us MORE than we need to fulfil His purpose in us.

Surely goodness and mercy shall follow me all the days of my life

It's not that hard to chase me. I am a fairly slow runner. You could catch me easily. Even if you were walking! But I know that I have sometimes made it harder for God to find me. The Bible tells us that God's goodness and His mercy come looking for us. Those parts of His nature chase us until they catch up with us.

At the moment Jon and I are leading an Alpha course and one

of our guests has described how this feels – as though God has been pursuing her for the last few years.

It is wonderful to remember that even when we make mistakes, even when we rush around in our frenetic busyness, even when we deliberately turn from the Lord, STILL, His goodness and His mercy are like some kind of love-seeking missiles. They are locked on to us as a target and won't rest until they catch up with us and bless us. However you feel today, it is important to remember that your holiness is not a failing project because it doesn't just depend on YOU. His goodness and His mercy may not have done their full work in you yet. But there is still time.

Have you ever stopped and just thanked God for His goodness? Have you ever come to a place where you have got on your knees and realised all His mercy and patience for you? There is a common call and response that many Christians say. The first part says, "God is good!" and it is followed by the answer, "All the time!" This is true and consistent with Scripture, but it is not the whole story! God is good, yes, but He is good to YOU. He is also good FOR you. He is GOODNESS personified. Perhaps you could take some time to praise Him for that right now?

When we know the true depth of the goodness of God, we can come to a genuine place of rest. We can be secure in the wisdom of His kindness and the knowledge of His care.

I shall dwell in the house of the Lord forever

Charles Spurgeon once said,

> "Some Christians try to go to heaven alone, in solitude. But believers are not compared to bears or lions or other animals

that wander alone. Those who belong to Christ are sheep in this respect, that they love to get together. Sheep go in flocks, and so do God's people."

There is something truly beautiful about gathering together as the people of God. Being in church is a source of great strength and gives my life so much meaning, stability and accountability. But this verse is not just about being in the house of the Lord NOW. It is a declaration about a future promise. It declares faith and trust in the truth and hope of eternity. Psalm 27:4 (NIV) says,

"One thing I ask from the LORD, this only do I seek: that I may dwell in the house of the LORD all the days of my life, to gaze on the beauty of the LORD and to seek him in his temple."

I am so excited that I will one day go to heaven! I am delighted that I will meet up with faithful people who have journeyed before me. I can't wait to see that "great cloud of witnesses", as it says in Hebrews 12, who have cheered me on. I can't tell you how delighted I will be to hug my mum and my grandparents! But SO much more than this, I am expectant and overjoyed to remember that I will one day meet my Jesus, face to face too.

As we have journeyed through this beautiful psalm, I hope you have been reminded of all you have been given in Jesus the Good shepherd. I pray that the knowledge of His love will enable you to take some rest and visit some green pastures and still waters of your own.

I will finish this chapter with a prayer from Hebrews 13:20-21:

"Now may the God of peace, who through the blood of the eternal covenant brought back from the dead our Lord Jesus, that great Shepherd of the sheep, equip you with everything good for doing his will, and may he work in us what is pleasing to him, through Jesus Christ, to whom be glory for ever and ever. Amen.

Rest Reflections:

- Is Jesus my shepherd?
- If He is, am I living as though I have all I need?
- In what ways do I need the truth of "still water" right now? What does that look like for me today?
- Am I still enough to see and hear what God has for me?
- Do I need to be reminded of any particular truth from Psalm 23? Which part blessed me the most? Why?
- Do I feel surrounded by enemies and attack at the moment? What comfort does this psalm give me today?
- What am I most looking forward to about heaven?

Chapter Eight
Give it a Rest

"We have to start breaking busy before the busy breaks us."
– Ali Worthington

An extract from my journal 4th Dec, 2006

"Today I went downstairs with a baby crying, leaving a baby crying and listening to a toddler crying. It was only me in the house. The job of mothering is one of constant choices – a series of mini-decisions. Shall I feed him? Is he tired? Did we clean his teeth? Is that yesterday's sick on the carpet?

This morning I breastfed one twin, whilst propping up the other with my feet and passing him the odd toy. I was also trying to buy a new tumble dryer on the phone from a monosyllabic 17-year-old (with attitude), to the unwelcome accompaniment of Sam banging two old biscuit tins with a biro and a piece of railway track. I am shattered."

Do I sound like a model of gentile calm?!

I was a very stressed mum of three boys under 2. I was desperately trying to prove to the world that I could handle them, even though most days my diary saw the truth that I was often lonely and struggling. I had to learn to be vulnerable with others and invite people into our loud and crazy world.

In theory, modern life makes it easier than ever to rest. We have more leisure time, more money and faster transportation than all of our ancestors. We own bread-makers, cappuccino frothers, hair dryers and cloud-based voice services. We rely on devices that can play us music, make calls, set alarms and timers, answer our questions, check our calendars, remind us to move, update us on weather, traffic and sports scores, manage our lists, control our compatible smart home devices, and generally think FOR us.

We should be the most rested generation EVER. But we know that as a nation our stress levels are high, our mental resources are low and our collective stamina and productivity waxes and wanes. We tend to be people who measure ourselves by our output, rather than our input. The pressure of modern life, and the fact that neither rest, nor resilience, has been modelled well to some of us, means we are truly in need of Jesus' example to us in these areas.

Rick Warren wrote, "The Bible is very clear that God put you here on Earth to do two things: to learn to love God and to learn to love other people. Life is not about acquisition, accomplishment or achievement." I can sometimes forget this.

I am a listy person. So listy that I sometimes keep lists of my lists. I take great pleasure in the creation of my lists and have been known to spend so long compiling and beautifying them, that I have no time left for accomplishing anything on them. Lists make me feel more efficient, even though I am regularly far from it.

Perhaps many of us can associate with writer Vaneetha Rendall Risner, who recently wrote,

"I'm ashamed to admit it, but a good day to me is defined by getting things accomplished on my list. Not the people I've touched. Not the time I've spent with God. Not the things I've learned. Just what I've done."

I am learning (slowly) that God doesn't place value on my life according to my capacity to tick off my activities. He gives me permission to rest. I find real resonance with Shauna Neiquist who said, "I don't want to get to the end of my life and look back and realise that the best thing about me was I was organised. That I executed well, that I ran a tight ship, that I never missed a detail."

There is so much more for us than this!

So how did Jesus rest? What can His life teach us?

The power of setting boundaries

We used to live in a picturesque little village in Kent, complete with its own cricket green. Every summer, a sweet man would mark out the crease and the boundary line with his ancient, squeaky white line marker and a set of ropes. He could just about see the lines from the year before and this helped him get the new lines in the correct place.

In cricket, a boundary line must be well-defined, or disputes may arise. Ropes are used at the edge of the pitch so that any balls bounce upwards, which is a useful indication of the score.

Clear boundary lines in our lives are so important. But for many of us they either don't exist or are incredibly vague. Jesus set boundaries around Himself regularly. We see this pattern in how He took time alone to be with God, drew Himself off to be with certain friends, and took deliberate rest. He was disciplined and focused with His time.

Psalm 16:5-8 (NIV) tells us something more about the beauty of boundary:

"Lord, you alone are my portion and my cup;
you make my lot secure.
The boundary lines have fallen for me in pleasant places;
surely I have a delightful inheritance.
I will praise the Lord, who counsels me;
even at night my heart instructs me.
I keep my eyes always on the Lord.
With him at my right hand, I will not be shaken."

Having good discipline in this way leads to a "delightful inheritance". Knowing what we are meant to achieve and what we can leave alone is incredibly freeing and helpful. This psalm reminds us that it is God's heart to instruct and counsel us and help us know what to do in life. This tells me something wonderful. Namely, *I don't have to do everything!* Rather, there are some things planned in advance for me to achieve (see Ephesians 2:10) and some things planned for others to accomplish.

One of my close friends, and a person of great and varied capacity, told me about how she and her husband set boundaries. She said, "As a family, we will take time to 'hibernate' and withdraw. We will say 'no' to very tempting social occasions to ensure we rest, spend time together as a family and don't run around like headless chickens. Sunday is very much our Sabbath and we tend to retreat as a family to rest and regroup on a Sunday afternoon."

How are your boundary lines? Are they clearly drawn for all to see, or do they need a re-think? Are you trying to achieve too much? Or are you someone who makes excuses and expects too little from your time?

The power of knowing who to reach

Jesus understood His mission. He was rarely found preaching to religious people in the Temple. He was not often in the presence of kings, rulers or statesmen. He spent the majority of His life with ordinary people, many of whom were from the lowest echelons of society. His stories and teachings were not set in theatres or on grand stages, but in houses, marketplaces, hillsides and lake shores.

Do you know who God has called you to?

One of my friends at university was a real high flyer. He knew he was called to reach business people in the City of London. Another of my friends knew she was being sent to Africa and another went to champion women's rights in Mexico. We are all so different!

Most of us have a part of society, a geographical place or a particular gifting that helps us work out who our main focus should be in any given season. Do you know yours? Are you reaching those people effectively?

The power of not hurrying

Jesus never seemed to live life in a tearing hurry, although He knew the preciousness of His time more than anyone. He was also constantly surrounded by needy, desperate people who all wanted His attention and energy. Much of the time we see the events of His days tumbling into one another as He preaches, casts out demons, heals a sick person and then speaks to a whole city – all in one day (as we see in Mark 1:21-34). John's Gospel tells us that there are many things Jesus did that were never even recorded. John 21:25 (NIV) says,

"Jesus did many other things as well. If every one of them were written down, I suppose that even the whole world would not have room for the books that would be written."

His life was full. And yet, Jesus had time for each person God put in His path.

Do I?

Do you?

Or are there sometimes people that get the thin end of our time and attention?

The power of being alone with God

Child diarist Anne Frank poignantly wrote, "The best remedy for those who are afraid, lonely or unhappy is to go outside, somewhere where they can be quite alone with the heavens, nature and God."

We read in Mark 1:35, and elsewhere in the New Testament, that life tired Jesus out. The result was not that He slept in and had lazy brunches on the beach, but that instead He got up early, while it was still dark and went to desolate places to pray. Jesus knew that this was what He needed most. Spending time alone with His father was the highest priority for Him. He knew the importance of revelation and heavenly direction. This pattern of going off alone is one that we see repeated throughout the four Gospels.

When we are most tired it is tempting to seek comfort in the warmth of the duvet. Perhaps what we need even more is the words of our Father over us?

The power of being with a few

After John the Baptist's death, in Mark 6:30-31 we read,

"The apostles gathered around Jesus and reported to him all they had done and taught. Then, because so many people were coming and going that they did not even have a chance to eat, he said to them, 'Come with me by yourselves to a quiet place and get some rest.'"

Jesus understands what His friends need. He sees that they are both physically and mentally shattered. They are grieving. He knows that they need time alone with Him and vice versa. We all need to protect time by ourselves with our best friends. This time feeds us and clothes us for what is to come.

There have been countless times in my life where Jon and I have gathered with our best pals and cried, laughed and prayed. Those precious hours have given us peace about the past, armed us with strength for the future, and given us stability for the present. I've found new perspective and peace when I have been around these people. We may not even talk about "my issues", but something about breathing the same air as them, listening to their spiritual vocabulary, learning from their journey and seeing their faith will often answer the cries of my heart.

When people know us well and love us deeply, their language will promote and animate us. What they dwell on will excite and engage us. What they've learned will teach and challenge us. It is important to surround yourself with those who can celebrate your capacity, not those who constantly question it or tell you are "trying to do too much". I have sometimes found that people who say that are often speaking from a place of unhealthy comparison, jealousy or fear.

Of course, there will be times when we DO take on too much and need to be guided by our families and friends to stop and rest. But we have to realise too that in different seasons, God will strengthen and widen our capacity through listening to the life-choices of others. No great achievement will happen by magic. It often takes hard work, tears and faithful prayer. Each of us have different strengths and levels of stamina. We also have unique giftings and mandates over our lives. It is key that we surround ourselves with people who support and scaffold whatever God has put within us.

Who are you trusting to lead you and bless you? Who gets to challenge you and offer you accountability? It is dangerous for your mental, physical and spiritual health to bury yourself away and cope with what you face alone. We all need a small number of close, life-affirming relationships to help us carry our callings to fruition.

The power of coming to Jesus
As I have quoted earlier *The Message* version of Matthew 11:28-30 is simple but profound. Here we read,

"Come to me. Get away with me and you'll recover your life. I'll show you how to take a real rest. Walk with me and work with me – watch how I do it. Learn the unforced rhythms of grace. I won't lay anything heavy or ill-fitting on you. Keep company with me and you'll learn to live freely and lightly."

What a wonderful offer that is! I want to keep company with Jesus and learn how to live free and light without anything heavy or ill-fitting on me. I love the fact that Jesus doesn't just offer us rest, but He shows us how much we will benefit from it. Resting with Him like this is not just an act of worship but a total gift.

Missionary Heidi Baker writes about how important our childlikeness is when we approach Jesus. She says,

"I have learnt over many years that I need to position myself well in order for God to use me. This means that I cannot waste my time worrying about how important I am, what people think of me or what my ambitions are.

Fortunately for us, we don't have to guess what Jesus requires of us in this area. The disciples were, at times, learning what He expected of them too. Matthew 18:1-5 (NIV) tells us,

At that time the disciples came to Jesus and asked, 'Who, then, is the greatest in the kingdom of heaven?' He called a little child to him, and placed the child among them. And he said: 'Truly I tell you, unless you change and become like little children, you will never enter the kingdom of heaven. Therefore, whoever takes the lowly position of this child is the greatest in the kingdom of heaven. And whoever welcomes one such child in my name welcomes me.'

Jesus is very clear here about how He expects us to behave and what He wants us to be like, isn't He? He is not asking us to try more, to work harder, or to court or catch more attention from others. He is asking us to become smaller.

I am learning to come to God small! He loves it when I position myself like this. Only when I realise that I can do nothing alone, can I achieve truly great things with Him."

The power of physical rest

The thunderstorm clapped terrifyingly over the house. Two of our little boys appeared next to me. I clutched them close to reassure them. As lightning filled the bedroom with flashes of light I had to smile. There was my Jon, totally fast asleep, peacefully snoring through it all!

One of the most incredibly human and yet supernatural stories we read about Jesus is found in Mark 4:35-41. The calming of the storm has never ceased to amaze me. Here, we see Jesus asleep on a cushion in the midst of a furious tempest. Jesus takes a nap in the middle of a crisis (don't you just love Him?!) He knew He was tired, BUT He also knew He was completely safe! I LOVE this!

This is a winning combination. The knowledge that I am tired AND safe allows me to rest. Sometimes we are ashamed of our tiredness. We try and stifle our yawns and hide our flu symptoms, sneak a Lemsip and carry on. But we need physical rest. Sometimes we need a proper, actual Jesus-style nap.

I know that for many people sleep during the day can seem like a weird luxury. It can even appear lazy. But it can be just what we need. Denying ourselves rest is not virtuous and can be an act of pride. And you know what? If Jesus did it, so can we.

I don't know what you are like when you are tired. When in need of rest I can be short-fused, prone to high emotion and unable to be truly grateful. God knows that I am not that nice to be around when I need sleep! So, He gave me permission, through this simple, short-but-true story, that even in the middle of crazy times in my life, to grab a pillow and get some decent z's in.

Are you in need of physical rest right now?

What are you doing about that?

The power of God-pleasing

Even when people were clamouring for Jesus, He sometimes chose to move away from them. Jesus was certain of God's call on His life and made sure that the crowds around Him didn't drive either His activity or His agenda.

I think most of us really struggle with this. If we see a problem we feel obliged to try to solve it ourselves. There are many times in our lives when other people's demands and ideas will chauffeur where we go, how we act and what we do.

I am slowly realising that God doesn't need my exhaustion in order to tick off His to-do lists in Heaven. He doesn't benefit much from my last-minute panics and frenzied stress. He, and just about everyone else in my life, gains far more from a rested, well-positioned and energised me.

Our good friend, who is an entrepreneurial businessman, told me that, for him, "Being effective in work means being well-rested and therefore being intentional about carving out time to rest." He continued, "This is part of our duty and responsibility, not only to those people we are working for, but also to ourselves to our families and most importantly God. We are no use to anyone burnt out!"

I couldn't agree more.

How can I live a more rest-filled life?
Now we have seen how Jesus operated, maybe there are some changes we need to make as we structure our time. We may do well to remind ourselves of the following declarations:

- **Principle of rest** – I need, deserve and am commanded to rest.
- **Prayer of rest** – I choose to come to Jesus, knowing that He is the source and giver of true rest.
- **Permission to rest** – I give myself space and permission to rest with all the options/choices that brings.
- **Preparation for rest** – I choose to look ahead at my year to prepare times when I will stop.

- **Planning to rest** – I will plan spaces to rest into my diary and make my colleagues, friends and family aware of those times.
- **Provision for rest** – I choose to put money or resources aside to help me rest creatively.
- **Protection rest brings** – I recognise that resting gives life and health to my soul and body and protects me from anxiety, depression and stress.

It might help to say these OUT loud. I just did it myself again and found it really empowering. You might feel a bit odd doing it. But it is great to say things we mean into the atmosphere we find ourselves in. So, go on, say it like you mean it!

"If you want to burn out and die young, no one will stop you; but if you want to live to a ripe old age, enjoy that life and be engaged and active throughout, it seems deliberate rest can help get you there." – Alex Soo-Jung Kim Pang

How to Do Less

Tim Kendall, CEO of Pinterest, wakes up each day and puts on a T-shirt saying the word "FOCUS" on it. (Before you ask, he has a number of the same shirts!) This practice started with a bet. He and a colleague decided to see who could wear the Focus T-shirt for the longest. He has been wearing his almost 5 years and clearly won the wager. The idea behind the statement comes from a simple belief. As Tim puts it, "Sometimes I'm not great at focusing, but if I put this shirt on every day, in a small part it reminds me that I need to stay focused and remember to say 'No' a lot, which I think most people – including myself – are not great at."

There is a huge amount of research dedicated to working less hours and being more effective in the process. New books such as Timothy Ferriss's *The 4-hour Work Week* give us tempting glimpses into a world of stress-free, hugely paid work and hours of play. I am not suggesting any kind of "get rich quick" scheme. But I do think some of us really need to think again about the patterns of the way we work and rest.

For example, studies into some of the most diverse and creative brains on the planet show how working only for short hours each day still achieves great results. Charles Dickens, for example, knew that his creativity was not the result of endless hours of toil. He worked a few solid hours in the morning, but what fuelled his thinking were the ten miles of walking he did every afternoon through the streets of London. Maybe this is what made his writing so vivid and contextually accurate. In this way, he wrote more than twenty-seven books.

Charles Darwin was another such man. He did four or five hours "deep" work a day and then walked, wrote letters, had a nap, walked again and had dinner. With this schedule, he completed nineteen books. His work was divided into three ninety-minute-periods each day. He is one of the most famous scientists in the world and yet it is almost certainly true that no university worth its salt would employ a man who kept those kind of working hours now!

Noted mathematician G.H. Hardy told a fellow Oxford professor, "Four hours creative work a day is about the limit for a mathematician."

It appears that sometimes less is MORE.

An Associate Professor of Computer Science at Georgetown University and the author of *Deep Work: Rules for Focused Success in a Distracted World*, Cal Newport, is a firm advocate of single tasking in which the worker commits at least 90 minutes to any task, putting it in the calendar and determining to complete it. In fact, single tasking, with breaks, is now thought to be the most scientifically effective way to get things done.

What does deep work or single tasking look like? It sounds fairly ruthless but I have found this to be very helpful to me:

- Setting boundaries on your work hours. For example, "I will only do 2 hours on my laptop today." Or, "I will only allow myself 15 minutes to clean the bathroom."
- Going to fewer meetings. Not every meeting is useful, interesting or purposeful. If you don't HAVE to be there, consider not going in order to protect work you DO have to do.
- Saying no to anything not within your calling and remit
- Cutting out anything that distracts you from your God-given goals.
- Keeping a record of deep work tasks that need completion.

Rest is not laziness

If we are doing what God has asked of us and are accountable to close, wise, godly friends, then we are not being lazy when we stop. Resting gives us energy and stamina. It helps us finish tasks and model God's effectiveness and creativity to others.

Writer, close friend and neighbour of Charles Darwin, John Lubbock, beautifully wrote,

"Rest is not idleness, and to lie sometimes on the grass under trees on a summer's day, listening to the murmur of the water, or watching the clouds float across the sky, is by no means a waste of time."

Proffesor Felicity Callard of Durham University, Director of Hubbub, says:

"We really need to challenge the assumption that if you take more rest, you are more lazy. The fact that people who are more rested seem to have better wellbeing is an endorsement of the need for the rest."

Resting helps us work harder, not less.
Resting is being like Jesus.

How do you rest with small children?

I am often asked how I get things done with all the children around me. One of the ways in which I operate is to go early to bed and rise early next day. I am not a night owl and am much more effective first thing in the morning. Occasionally, I wake up very early indeed, especially when I am in the middle of a project, such as writing a talk or a book. If I feel awake enough I will get up and start my day, even if it is 4 or 5am. I don't need quite as much sleep as I used to. I start my day reading my Bible in bed. Jon is also an early waker and he brings me a hot drink sometime after 6am.

I get the vast majority of my tasks done first thing. For example, I tend to cook, or at least prepare our main meal, before or around breakfast. I am just so much faster in my thinking and actions then. It takes me half the time to sort a meal at that hour of the day. I don't enjoy cooking when the kids are doing their homework and need my help and attention later in the day. I take great comfort in knowing that a Cottage Pie – or whatever – is all ready to go when they get home from school. I have a menu plan, so I am not having to think about what to cook. I know what I have planned in advance, so it's almost robotic to just do it. Once this particular job is done I find it gives me a lot more thought-room for work, play or rest. When the kids were really small, I would sometimes make batch meals or cook before I went to bed, so that it was ready for the following day.

As I have said earlier, I am very list-driven. I have things I try to achieve each day. But, rather more unusually perhaps, I also keep lists of thing I have to look forward to, treats in store, so that I can enjoy thinking about those things too.

You might say to me, "I am a busy parent. How do I do ANY of those things?!" As a mum of four, I know what it feels like to go without lots of things I want in order to sacrifice time and energy for my kids. I know that it is hard work. Let me just offer a few simple suggestions for you that might give you some ideas:

Rest when they do. When your baby/child or children nap or have down time, do it too. You can always put the washing on when they are around and let them help/watch/dribble near you. Don't rush around emptying bins or hoovering when they are asleep. Lie down too.

Prayer. Giving things over to God has the absolutely amazing side effect of making us more effective people. As well as reducing our stress, prayer makes us more compassionate, more self-aware, more forgiving, more peaceful and more centred. Prayer gives us fresh perspectives on our problems and dilemmas. It also gives us access to Heavenly creativity and wisdom.

Quiet times. Try and have quiet activities like jigsaws, playdough or reading time for your kids after lunch. When mine were younger, I found it useful to gather some quiet toys and books in a pillow case and hang it (using the fold) on the back of a chair. That way those things were close to hand as soon as I'd scooped the sandwich crumbs from all the highchairs/floor.

Routine. Both children and adults can find routine more restful than spontaneity. Try and get your day into a routine that suits you. Do a nappy change or face wash to signify the end of the meal and the start of a different or quiet time. I even had a silly little song I used to sing that helped my kids to know what we were going to do next.

Change your mood. Being on your own with small children is rewarding, but can be exhausting. I used to have days when I felt quite low. I found (and still find now) that I can change my mood with smells and sound. For me the scent of candles and the sound of certain music can often melt away my frustrations. Just lighting a candle and giving yourself a different scent in the room can calm you (and your little ones) down and help you breathe deeply. Let's face it, children don't always smell sweet and wonderful! So, a little perfume in the room can really help you feel a bit more human again. I now also use a grapefruit room spray to lift my mood and freshen the room. Most evenings I light candles (in a safe place) to signify a different, quieter part of the day. It's my way of saying to myself and others, "I expect less of myself from now on today. We are winding down."

Keep ideas handy. Have an ideas list on the fridge or somewhere you can see it easily. This is for when you are truly exhausted and can't think of activities to do. Things like singing time, stories, construction, art, going to the park, Facetime Auntie Claire, or whatever would work for your family. This has been a life-saver for me, especially when I have been up all night with teething twins.

Good food. Treat yourself to something tasty and healthy to eat. As a younger mum, I was often very tired and didn't always eat well. I ate a lot of "what was right *there*", rather than "what was right". The older I get, the more I am realising that eating crisps won't help me. I won't feel fresh and satisfied afterwards. I will feel a bit greasy and unhealthy. I know so many parents who miss out on eating well because they are busy doing other things.

Putting a pretty, simple salad in a mason jar or bit of Tupperware when you are having breakfast takes seconds, but feels like a life-saver later in the day. I would often prepare lunch on our little indented dinner trays for my kids too and cover it with cling film. Then at any time when I felt they were hungry (sometimes as early at 11.15am!) I would whip it out of the fridge, whack it on the table, place my three kids in their high chairs and feel like a domestic goddess – for four whole seconds anyway.

I NEVER eat at my desk. However busy I am, I will always have a lunch break and stop. I have learnt how good it is for me and the kids to take stock, rethink and rest at the table, or have a floor picnic halfway through the day. I know I need to eat the right things at lunch time. I know that many parents find themselves falling into the bad habit of having little, or even no food at all. Trying to "get stuff done" has become a byword for "neglecting ourselves". We know (deep down) that our bodies need healthy nutrition. But how many times have we gone without what our Nan would call a "proper lunch" and thrown down a cup of cold coffee and a stale museli bar instead?

I think we often forget that failing to give ourselves a decent meal will negatively impact our brain and body's productivity for the rest of the day. It will also make us less patient with our little ones. Of course, we all know that the opposite is true too. Eating a heavy, carb-tastic lunch is likely to have you nodding off in a corner of the playroom.

One thing I got almost addicted to as a young mum was carrot sticks. They were my saving grace. I made a massive batch of them at the start of the week and put them in different sandwich bags to be ready each day. If you make or buy some yummy humous or dips, that is a great snack or addition to lunch. Olives, nuts, blueberries – anything fun and fresh would be a good idea. Prepping food in advance is always a boon. If you focus on fresh food, whole grains, vegetables and fruits, you will feel better for longer.

Switch off. Depending on your body clock, your natural energy levels are lower around 2pm – making that the perfect time for a little 20-minute lie down/down time. You may not be able to actually sleep – especially if your babies/toddlers are climbing on your face – but how about switching off for a while? You could turn off your laptop or stop for a while. Read a book, avoid social media and stay off your phone. Naps can help us remember what we need to focus on. Sleep helps us clear away the information we no longer need from the morning. Having chance to unwind and recharge means our stress levels stay low and that takes away tension, anxiety and worry.

Stop thinking. Taking a short break from making the thousands of tiny decisions we need to when working or caring for others is so good for you! If you feel as though you are not being as effective as you could be, it might be that your brain is simply overloaded and needs a break. Try it! I love to get into a good book or a lovely magazine. Escaping and becoming absorbed in reading can be such a break from the normality of your four walls and can help your mind unwind.

Exercise. Lunch time is a great space to go for a walk or a run. Exercise reduces stress, improves our mood and boosts our metabolism and self-esteem. It doesn't have to be long. It just has to be sustained for 20-30 minutes. Plus, you will feel like some kind of exercise guru/ninja all afternoon if you work out over lunch. Just remember to eat and drink too! If you have a small child, bundle them into a buggy and take them out for some fresh air with you. Or, failing that, do a DVD in the lounge and pop your child into a baby bouncer or on a floor mat. If none of that is possible, stretch your body purposefully and roll your shoulders to stop yourself feeling stiff and sore.

Drink water. So many people are less efficient because their bodies are thirsty. Often, we mistake the cue of thirst for hunger and eat instead. The NHS recommend that adults drink 6-8 glasses of water a day (the equivalent of 2 litres). If you feel sleepy in the afternoon, try downing fresh, cold water before you try anything else. Drinking water helps to regulate our body temperature, aids us in circulating nutrients and clears the skin and mind.

Be still. Sometimes it's nice to be sociable and go out for a chatty, fun lunch with other kids and parents. But there are some days when your mind and body are craving stillness and peace. Try and pace your week and see what your heart needs most.

Write stuff down. Your head can only hold so much information. Find a notebook or piece of paper that you can tumble your thoughts onto. Once they are written down you no longer have to store them and that can feel restful.

Create. As we have said in earlier chapters, making or creating something can help us rest. My friend is Assistant Director in a very busy council. She is also a bestselling author of crochet and knitting designs. She says, "My knitting and crochet is a very important part of my 'rest-routine'. It allows me to sit. I do *a lot* of processing and subconscious thinking whilst my hands are working the yarn. It means that my mind is rested from the thoughts and responsibilities of my other work."

I know that when I make something, whether that be a casserole or a card, something in me begins to slow down and rest. Being creative allows space for reflection and brings us the gift of absorbing time in a different way.

How do you rest as a carer?
Resting when you are also a carer is especially challenging. Our friends Dan and Lucy have three beautiful children. One of them, Rufus, has Angelman syndrome. This means he has developmental delay, difficulty walking and balancing and minimal speech sounds. He also has a happy, excitable personality and frequently smiles and laughs and gives THE most amazing bear hugs! Rufus is adorable and everyone who meets him, loves him. But, caring for him can be tiring and demanding. I asked Lucy how she and Dan rest.

Lucy said, "We lean into our village a lot. If people offer to help, we take them up on it. If that means to have Rufus for a few hours we jump on it. Also, we have lowered our expectations of a lot of things outside of basic family life. This is the hardest bit, as we can't be the hosts we want to be; we can't be as spontaneous as we would love to be. We know we can't be at everything and do everything. We also can't massively give ourselves to other people or serve at church in the way we have in the past. We still see ourselves as needing to accept help wherever its offered. But, being part of such an awesome church means we can just rest in knowing we are being carried sometimes."

There is such wisdom here. The role Dan and Lucy share carries obvious sacrifices, but there is both a deep acceptance and a huge joy that this is what they are consistently called to as a family.

You may be caring for a child or an elderly relative full time. Getting support so that you can take some much-needed time out is vital. When I had three very young children I was entitled to some council help once a week. Even a couple of hours of having another person to come and visit me was amazing. There is local support out there for you. Get some advice from your GP, your church, or your local Citizens Advice Bureau.

Like Lucy said so beautifully, when my babies were young, I had to learn to "lean in" and trust my church family to help me too. My immediate family were also amazing – especially when my children were first born. My parents faithfully came every day (except Wednesday) from 7am-7pm for the first 8 months after the twins were born. And on Wednesday's, Jon's parents arrived for the same time period! Now that the children are older and my wider family has changed shape and moved away, I rely even more fully on my church friends to support me with our daily life. If one of the children is ill or struggling, or I need support in some way, I know that our friends will be there like a shot. I know there is a large group of people praying for us, loving us and wanting the best for us. We form part of that network for them too. I love the privilege of being asked to pick up other people's children from school, care for them on days when their parents are working, or make meals for those in need. Community like this is invaluable.

Sabbaticals

In the digital age where we are connected to everything and everyone, we are constantly being distracted, interrupted and disrupted. That gets wearing on the soul. But just because we are busy doesn't mean we are accomplishing the right things. We often mistake activity for achievement. But they are NOT the same.

A sabbatical (from the Hebrew word *Shabbat*) literally means a "ceasing" from work. Described in several places in the Bible this rest is a total break from labour. Every seven years, the Jewish people would cancel debts and let the land rest for a year. In more recent times, a Sabbatical has come to mean an extended time away from work – usually agreed with colleagues and bosses – in order to achieve something specific. But in Nehemiah 10:31 (NIV) we see its origins:

> "When the neighbouring peoples bring merchandise or grain to sell on the Sabbath, we will not buy from them on the Sabbath or on any holy day. Every seventh year we will forgo working the land and will cancel all debts."

This was a time when the land could regain its potency and when people were given a fresh start. In the same way, a sabbatical is a time when someone can rediscover what they are passionate about and hungry for. It is time to generate new sources of spiritual nutrition and find new insight.

Designer Stefan Sagmeister is a key figure in advertising. He has huge, high-profile clients and yet every seven years he takes a WHOLE year off. Yes, you read that right. A whole year!

Stefan said,

"I myself had several reasons to start the first sabbatical: one was to fight routine and boredom, another the insight that I could come up with different kinds of projects when given a different time-frame to spend on them. I also expected it would be joyful. What I did not expect was that these sabbaticals would change the trajectory of the studio, and I did not dare to imagine that they would be financially successful. But they were."

He later told an interviewer that taking sabbaticals was the best business idea he had ever had. How incredible is that?

Studies into those who have sabbaticals have found a huge improvement in family connection, physical and mental health and wellbeing, as well as work-life balance. A 2009 study found that three quarters of those interviewed said that they were able to crystallise or frame a new vision for their organisations as a result. Sabbaticals give us the chance to redefine our vision and check that we are living by the rules we care about most.

You might say to me that you haven't got a spare year of your life when you can down tools and stop working and earning! Perhaps you couldn't name a time when you could pop off to a "Think Week" cabin by seaplane. And you may also be keen to tell me that you don't currently have a chef who could cook you two meals a day and leave you to it. Nor have I! But I could take a couple of weekends out, to totally stop, maybe at a friend's house when they are away, to give me space and quiet. Sabbaticals and retreats don't necessarily need to have huge expense attached, but they do need forward planning and time.

Is this something you could book into your life soon?

For the rest of your life
So many of us strive for perfection. As we have said before in this book, we rush around, trying our hardest to hold it all together. But this is so detrimental for our hearts. As Shauna Niequist wrote, "What kills a soul? Exhaustion, secret keeping, image management. And what brings a soul back from the dead? Honesty, connection, grace."

Psalm 62:5 says, "Let all that I am wait quietly before God, for my hope is in Him." Many of us try and complicate it. But rest is actually pretty simple. It is about waiting quietly and putting our hope where it belongs – in HIM.

As we come to the end of this book together I will leave you with a word of comfort from Hebrews 13:5 (AMPC)

"...Be satisfied with your present [circumstances and with what you have]; for He [God] Himself has said, I will not in any way fail you nor give you up nor leave you without support. [I will] not, [I will] not, [I will] not in any degree leave you helpless nor forsake nor let [you] down (relax My hold on you)! [Assuredly not!]"

It could be that you have read through this book and simply feel ready to stop trying so hard. You might want to release everything back to the One who loves you and will not, as we have just read, ever relax His hold on you. If that sounds like it is resonating in your heart, this is a prayer, just for you.

———

A Prayer for a Weary Soul

Lord, I give you the full, weighty burden of my tiredness. It is so heavy. I feel at the end of my resources. I am stretched out of shape and don't like what I see. I pray that you would help me to find rest in your presence and your promises and be brave enough to stay there for a while. Fill the parts of me that are empty and dry. Remove the fake or the perceived need to impress or dress up my life in front of you.

I ask that you would teach me true rest. Help me discover new ways to be myself. Help me explore and create fresh pathways of calm. Please help this next season be one charactierised by my re-creation. I pray that I might find peace, even in the most trying situations and that I might be someone who is found faithful and unwavering. Help me navigate the chaos of my life in a way that brings deeper trust in your guidance.

Teach me to honour stopping and not glorify my personal busyness any longer.

Amen.

———

You are so loved and so valued by God. You don't have to try and prove your worth to Him any longer. I pray you would know that. For the rest of your life.

With love,

Ems

Rest Reflections:

- Do I have enough alone-time with God?
- Do I feel my relationship with God is artificial or authentic?
- Take another look at the declarations mentioned earlier.

Principle of rest – I need, deserve and am commanded to rest.

Prayer of rest – I choose to come to Jesus, knowing that He is the source and giver of true rest

Permission to rest – I give myself space and permission to rest with all the options/choices that brings.

Preparation for rest – I choose to look ahead at my year to prepare times when I will stop.

Planning to rest – I will plan spaces to rest into my diary and make my colleagues, friends and family aware of those times.

Provision for rest – I choose to put money or resources aside to help me rest creatively.

Protection rest brings – I recognise that resting gives life and health to my soul, and body and protects me from anxiety, depression and stress.

- Which of these declarations do I need God's wisdom on?
- Which of them do I need to action in some way?
- What can I do to make that happen?

For more information, or to access Ems's blog and other books, please make your way to:

http://www.emshancock.com

or to

http://www.river-publishing.co.uk

About Ems...

Ems Hancock is a speaker and author based in South Manchester. She is married to Jon who is a TV producer. They have four children under thirteen.

Ems' passion is to see people freed to live the way they were intended to. She spends most of her time bringing up the children, writing, and running a listening service in a local secondary school. She and her husband have recently joined a small team to plant a new church as part of the Ivy network of churches. You can find out more about her at: www.emshancock.com